A Discourse of Trade

In Two Parts

The first treats of the Reason of the Decay
of the Strength, Wealth, and Trade of ENGLAND

The latter, of the Growth and Increase of the
DUTCH Trade above the ENGLISH

ROGER COKE

RE-ISSUED IN A SERIES OF REPRINTS OF
CLASSIC ENGLISH WORKS ON
THE HISTORY AND DEVELOPMENT OF
ECONOMIC THOUGHT,
UNDER THE EDITORIAL DIRECTION OF
PROFESSOR W. E. MINCHINTON
UNIVERSITY OF EXETER

S. R. PUBLISHERS LIMITED
JOHNSON REPRINT CORPORATION

This reproduction has been made with the kind permission of the Goldsmiths' Librarian, University of London, from the copy held in the Goldsmiths' Library, Senate House, London, W.C. 1.

The publishers would like to acknowledge the assistance of Dr. J. H. P. Pafford, M.A., F.S.A., F.L.A., the former Goldsmiths' Librarian, Miss M. B. C. Canney of the Goldsmiths' Library and Mr. F. J. Bosley, M.I.R.T., the chief photographer to the Goldsmiths' Library, without whose assistance this series of reprints could not have been successfully undertaken.

Library of Congress Catalog Card Number: 70-114073

British Standard Book Number: 85409-241-2

S. R. Publishers Ltd.
East Ardsley, Wakefield
Yorkshire, England

Johnson Reprint Corporation
111 Fifth Avenue
New York, N. Y. 10003, U.S.A.

Printed in the U.S.A.

A

DISCOURSE

OF

TRADE.

In two Parts.

The first treats of
The Reason of the Decay of the Strength,
Wealth, and Trade of *ENGLAND*.

The latter,
Of the Growth and Increase of the *Dutch*
Trade above the *English*.

By *ROGER COKE*.

LONDON,
Printed for H. *Brome*, at the Gun near the *West-End*
of St. *Pauls* : and R. *Horne* at the South Entrance of
the *Royal Exchange*, *Cornhill*, 1670.

To the great Example of Virtue

Sir CHARLES HARBORD.

SIR,

IF I could defcribe Trade in all its excellencies, fo well as *Ben. Johnfon* does the mind, and were to prefent it to him who I thought did know beft how to value it, I would prefer Sir *Charles Harbord*: For in him befides a well weighed underftanding, it will meet with an open and free accefs (which are the principles from whence Trade is beft generated, preferved, and increafed) conjoyned with fo even a temper, that he is never moved to judge, or act, but from caufes before underftood by him.

This, Sir, is one reafon why this Treatife implores your Patronage ; and I wifh that the fame method of reafoning were obferved in Geometry, Numbers, Divinity, Phyfick, and Natural Philofophy, as in this Difcourfe, *viz.* firft to eftablifh the principles, and by a certain rule to reafon under them. The principles from which all Learning and Reafoning are gene- *Anal. poft. l 8.* rated are three (though *Ariftotle* is pleafed to reftrain *c. 32. lit. 12.* them to two) *viz.* Definitions, or fenfible things or actions before known, which cannot be defined ; Petitions, and Axioms or Common Notions. Here you may be pleafed to take notice how by not right underftanding the nature of thefe Principles, and confounding them, all Learning and Reafoning in thefe ftudies is rendred perplexed, difficult, and uncertain, and without any Order or Method ; which that I may

avoid,

avoid, I think fit here to declare the nature of them, and how they differ from one another.

A Definition is the explaining the name of ſome intelligible thing or act, which may be underſtood, but cannot be the object of ſence, nor can be taken for a Propoſition. Senſible things and actions may be alike known to ſenſitive Creatures, who have like ſences: but definitions are only underſtood by intelligent Creatures, never to ſenſitive. For example, a Man, a Tree, a Horſe, or any ſenſible thing may be alike perceived by all ſenſitive Creatures, who have like ſences. But Father, Merchant, Lawyer, Point-line, &c. may be defined and underſtood by intelligent Creatures, but can never be perceived by ſenſitive. By no power of the underſtanding can any man, negatively void of any ſence, be made to perceive any thing which is ſubject to that ſence. A man negatively blind, cannot be made to perceive things which are only viſible, nor deaf to perceive ſounds which are only audible; and ſo it is of the other ſences. And as in Things, ſo in Actions; carnal copulation, killing another, and taking from another, are ſenſible Actions, and cannot be defined: but Murder, Juſtice, Adultery, Theft, &c. may be defined and underſtood by intelligent creatures, but can never be perceived by the ſences, or ſenſitive Creatures. How much time is loſt, and confuſion cauſed in defining ſenſible things by *Ariſtotle*, *Plato*, and our Schools, which every ignorant man knows as much as the moſt learned; and a thouſand times better than all theſe Sophiſters by their contention in them, I leave to you Sir to judge.

To this loſs of time in defining ſenſible things, *Ariſtotle* and our Schools from him, do not only confound
defini-

definitions with propofitions ; fometimes giving a definition the power of a particular propofit on, other times of an univerfal ; but he makes a man to be an univerfal propofition, and the man *Callias* to be a particular : Nor is *Euclid* wholly free from miftaking herein ; for he oftentimes confounds definitions with propofitions, as hereafter fhall be fhewed. So as *Clavius* following the Authority of *Ariftotle* and *Euclid*, and attempting t> Analyfe the Propofitions of *Euclid* in a rational method, not only makes the Comment more perplexed and tedious, but not otherways to be done ; which is the reafon he fays in his Scholium upon the firft Propofition of the firft Book of *Euclid*, that you muft take the way he is forced to do, as well as others before him.

2. Petitions are immediate Propofitions, wherein is propounded fome certain knowledge, which is either underftood to be neceffary in one or more of the definitions, or fome fenfible thing or act before known ; or 2dly. you require that one or more of the definitions, or acts may be expreffed , or done by every learner ; or laftly fact or defect may be propounded in one or more of them, which muft be unqueftionably true, as it is propounded : Thefe are frequently confounded by Commentators upon *Euclid*, with Axioms and common Notions. So, Sir, as it is no wonder that no method or rule of reafoning is obferved in Geometry, where the principles of it are fo perplexed and confounded ; whereby *Urania*, fo far and lovely in it, is fo clouded, and all ways of approaching her fo obftructed ; that of ingenious men , who defire to pay their Oblations at her Altars , not one of twenty can find the paffage to her.

3. But

3. But these principles are so sterile, that without the conjunction of a superiour and nobler cause they are never impregnated with any new generation of knowledge. Nor can this knowledge be begotten from any less power than that which is eternal and necessary in all things or actions, as they are propounded. These principles from their excellency are stiled Axioms, Dignities, Universals, and Common Notions ; and though every acquired proposition hath the authority of a Petition, yet by no learning or reason can any Proposition have the authority of an Axiom.

The principles thus established, men begin to learn and reason, whereby knowledge may be infinitely improved by reason, but never the principles ; for as *Aristotle* in very many places affirms, they are indemonstrable, and the intellect without reason, is of them, and reason is of conclusions deduced from them. Here, Sir, I cannot pass over the first stumble which is laid before every learner in our vu'gar Logick, which in the first page affirms Logick to prove (not the consequences but) the Principles in its own Science and others too : which is all one, as if one says the consequences (which must ever be proved by the premisses) go before the principles, and the principles and premisses come after the consequences and conclusions. So as not only all rules of reasoning are hereby inverted and destroyed, but the authority of *Aristotle* contemned, who as I remember, in 16 places of his Analyticks, and frequently in his Physicks, Metaphysicks, Topicks, and Ethicks, affirms the principles of Science to be indemonstrable ; and that reason is of Science, and demonstrable : And sure it is great pity none of the Rabbines correct it : though from no learning or autho-

authority of *Ariſtotle* or our vulgar Logick was ever any progreſs of knowledge in any one propoſition acquired or heard of, I am ſure not by me.

Theſe principles thus eſtabliſhed, this method or rule muſt be obſerved in the generation of knowledge. One or more of the definitions, or things, or actions before known (which are termed the ſubjects of the propoſition) muſt be aſſumed in every ſcientifical propoſition, either ſimply or conditionally, wherein either ſome thing or act is propounded to be done (which is termed a Problem) which was not before known in any of the petitions or demonſtrated propoſitions, or ſome new knowledge in the Subjects propounded (which is termed a Theorem) which was not before known: & in the demonſtration of this thing to be done or knowledge to be underſtood (which are termed the Queſtions of the Propoſition.) The major propoſition muſt be an Axiom, the minor propoſition ſo made up of the Petitions, and before demonſtrated propoſitions, and the Hypotheſis, if the Subjects be conditionally aſſumed, conformable in all parts to the major propoſition, that the affirmation or queſtion of the propoſition, or the contradiction, if the demonſtration be negative, may flow into the concluſion.

Here, Sir, be pleaſed to ſtay a little, and behold rational knowledge thus begotten, how fair and lovely ſhe is in her pure and ſimple nakedneſs! how pleaſant and eaſie are her ways? and how excellent and noble is her extraction? deſcended from eternal cauſes: begotten by a mind ſo pure, as partakes not any affection of any ſenſual appetite or paſſion: Her ways all plain and before known, and may be apprehended as well by youth of both Sexes as men of riper years.

Nor

Nor does knowledge thus begotten by the mind die
with the body ; but though fhe be the daughter of
time, remains an eternal monument of the minds excel'ency, being fubject to no alteration, wrimple, or
decay by any power of time or fate. Oh Divine knowledge ! how is thy excellency impofed upon by Pride,
Affectation, Vain glory. and hard Words ? How are
thy ways obftructed by Faction, Prejudice, and Self-
intereft ? Whilft thy glorious beauty is never confpi-
cuous, but by denying thefe, and frequenting the hum-
bleft paths.

If, Sir, I have more than becomes me infifted upon
your patience, I am fo far from excufing my felf
herein, that I acknowledge I have often before done it,
with this advantage to my felf, that as well in this as
many other things I have had the honour to be confirmed by your more difcerning Judgment. This
Treatife therefore prefumes to infcribe your Name,
whereby it well hopes to be enlivened when its own
little worth fhall find no other Monument: fo, Sir, I
defire you to entertain a belief of me, that no man
more truly honours you, or wifhes you more happi-
nefs than,

SIR,

Your moft devoted and

obedient Servant

Roger Coke.

PREFACE
TO THE
READER.

GOD hath endued other Creatures besides Man The Nature with Sense, Appetite and Fear; so as excited by of Man. their Appetite, and directed by their Senses, without any subordination of one to another, they pursue and attain those things, which Nature had before provided for their subsistence; and prompted by their innate impulse of fear, they avoid and flee from those Creatures and things, which are Enemies and hurtful to them. But the case is otherwise with Man, for God hath endued him with a Higher and Nobler Faculty of Soul, in giving him understanding, which by Reason, not Love, Hatred, Fear, or Desire, Governs all his Actions: for where these or any of them prevail, those men never understand, judg, or act aright. And Men, not as other creatures, live in Society and Subordination: So that under the Laws of God, and their Superiors, men eat their bread in the sweat of their brows. Nature of her own accord hath ordained subsistence necessary for other creatures: Whereas though God hath made all things for the use of Man, yet nothing is useful to Man (pure Water, Milk, and some of the fruits of the earth in their seasons excepted) but as it is prepared by Humane Art and Industry. While other Creatures live free and Independent from one another, only Man stands in need and help of another: And therefore where things are best prepared for Humane necessities and convenience, there Necessity of men most resort: from whence Humane Society, Industry and Civi- Trade. lity, is improved above those places where these are not, and men but few.   And

Preface to the Reader.

And this is so well understood, that Trade is now become the
Lady, which in this present Age is more Courted and Celebrated than in any former by all the Princes and Potentates of the
World, and that deservedly too; For she acquires not her Dominion by the Horrid and Rueful face of Warr, whose footsteps
leave ever behind them deep impressions of misery, devastation,
and poverty, but with the pleasant aspect of wealth and plenty
of all things conducing to the benefit of Humane life and Society,
accompanied with strength to defend her, in case any shall attempt
to Ravish or Invade her.

Take an Instance or two herein. When the United Netherlands
made their defection from the Crown of Spain, Spain was in its
greatest height and riches; after some Commotions, ten of the Provinces did either return or were subdued to the Crown of Spain;
yet the other seven for neer 40 years together, by Warr and Policy maintained themselves against all the Power of Spain, untill the charge became so insupportable to the Crown of Spain,
that Philip the Second, about the year 1607. was forced to
seek a Truce from the States, and afterward in the year 1648.
Philip the Fourth, a Peace. Yet all this Warr was maintained
by these States purely upon the account of Trade, and that
Forein; for other means all the World knows they had none:
And though they were constantly assisted by Queen Elizabeth
and the French Kings successively, yet were all the Forces of
England and France as constantly paid by the States. In our
late Warrs with them, notwithstanding the extraordinary sup-
plyes imployed upon that occasion, and the losses susteined by the
Dutch incomparably more than were the English, yet this Nation by experience found, that the Dutch upon the Account of
their Trade supported the Charge of the Warr against all diffi-
culties. The Bounds set by Warr are Towns, Forts and Castles,
whereas neither Land nor Ocean put any Period to the Jurisdi-
ction of Trade.

The English and Dutch have of late by a furious Warr contended who should enjoy her, but whilest these Covetous Combatants contend so fiercely for her, the French King by all the Modes
of France Courts her for himself; yet this, though Covertly carryed, was perceived by some of the jealous Combatants, who had rather

ther enjoy her, neither can tell how, than wholly lose her to their Powerful and Courtly Neighbour.

But Warr is not the Mean by which this Lady may be won; for though she be pleased to be Guarded by Arms, yet will she never admit to be governed by them; therefore if either English or Dutch had subdued other; yet should not Trade have longer continued with either, than men observe the Rules and Method by which it may be advanced more than in any other Place, which hath equal conveniences.

If this Lady were to choose an habitation in all the known World, she could not find any so capable of her reception as England, (I had almost said and Ireland) whether it be in regard of the Multitude, Excellency, and Conveniency of our Ports: Abundance of Wool better than in any other place of the World, but Segovia, and from us they had it: Cattle of all sorts equal, if not superior to any other place: More Horses, and more serviceable in Trade than any where else: Timber for shipping the best in the World: Lead, Tin, Seacoal, and Fullers Earth, not to be found out of England, so much, or so Good: and capable of all other things but Wines, (and we were better without them) which may any ways conduce to the supplying the necessities, or adorning the convenience of Humane life, equal with any other place. The Coast enriched with a shore more worth than the King of Spains West-Indies: The Inhabitants stout and valiant, accompanied with a lively wit and healthful constitution, and generaly disposed to her service.

One would think it strange (I might say monstrous) that the Dutch Nation, who are denied these advantages, and are of a more dull and heavy constitution than the English, should out-wit us in that wherein God and Nature have given us all the Prerogatives we our selves can desire. But we undo our selves by banishing this Lady we so desire and contend for; she is already so farr withdrawn, that we neither know where to find her, nor much better how to recover her.

Though this beloved Lady is become very Coy to us by Land; yet in reason we hope to prevail upon her by Sea. In our application we tell her, the Swelling Ocean every day beats round about

our

Preface to the Reader.

our *Shores, to invite us to the enjoyment of her; and that by a long and uninterrupted series of Ages we have been possessed of her before ever the* Dutch *Government was formed into States.*

We have moreover in the year 1662, contributed several considerable sums of Mony toward the Advancement of the Fishing Trade; but how the Monies have been disposed of, and whether the Monies Collected be not yet in the Collectors hands unaccounted for, may be worthy Consideration; especially considering how great a discouragement it will be to all Publique undertakings, when such benevolences are diverted from their designed end.

Many men not understanding the Reason of this Ladies strangeness to us of late, have ascribed it to two causes, viz. that we Import more than we Export; and that men generally live above their Estate; but neither of these, though true, are Reasons of the decay of Trade; for the Dutch we see Import all, yet thrive upon Trade, and the Irish Export eight times more than they Import, yet grow poorer. And Trade if it be well managed, no where thrives better than where men spend above the ordinary means of living.

We have lost the Trade upon the matter by Sea and Land at home; but before we demonstrate from what causes, or propound any Expedients by which we may be relieved, let us see how it stands abroad: We have lost the Trade to Muscovy, and so have that to Greonland, the Trade to Norway possessed by the Norwegians, and the Reasons given in to the Parliament last Sessions: The Trade to Guinney driven by a few, and exclusive to other men: The Spanish and Turkey Trades abated, and in danger: So that unless it be in the French and Canary Trades, wherein we undo our selves, we are making hast to betake our selves to our Plantations only, yet shall not be long able to continue that Trade for want of shipping.

By what accident England of late became so rich.

It is true indeed, that England of late under King James, but more especially under King Charles did flourish by Trade, and was more Rich than any other Kingdom in these Western Parts of the World; but this was by an Accident of the Times, not to be again hoped for: For the Austrian Family under Maximilian the Second, and Philip the Second, attained to that Power and Riches,

when

Preface to the Reader.

when the Netherlands made their defection from the Crown of Spain, that it was not only formidable to the Great Turk, but to all the Christian Princes of Europe; Queen Elizabeth therefore and the French Kings successively openly assisted them in their defection: But Philip the Second dying, and Queen Elizabeth soon after, King James and Philip the Third, in the beginning of their Reigns made Peace, which continued neer 40 years with little Interruption. During which the Warrs continued between the United Netherlands and Spain, with little Intermission; whereby the English became Proprietors of the Trade with Spain, and by consequence great sharers in the Wealth of the West-Indies. And this Benefit moreover the English reaped by these Warrs, that the Merchant supplied the Spanish Netherlands with Commodities; and both Spanish and United Netherlands were supplied with Souldiers from England, whereby many of them on both sides, especially Officers acquired much Wealth.

But the Nation, not content to enjoy Peace, Riches and Plenty above any other Nation, brought upon itself all the miseries and Calamities incident to a Civil Warr, so that Regal Power, as to the exercise of it, for neer 20 years together was suspended; during which, in the year 1648. the Dutch made Peace with Spain, and Oliver in the year 1654. brake with it (which was a folly never to be forgiven in his Politicks, nor the losses this Nation susteined thereby, ever again to be repaired) whereby the Condition of the English and Dutch in reference to the Trade with Spain became quite inverted; and this continuing neer seven years, the Dutch are so good Masters of Trade, that little hopes is left the English of Enjoying it as before. ^{From what cause it lost its Riches.}

From hence it is, which being past cannot be helped; and for the Reasons in this Discourse which may be helped, and for other Causes which only God in his goodness can help: From hence it is, I say, that this Kingdom becomes decayed in Trade, and must every day degenerate into worse, unless some such Reformation be made, with Gods great blessing upon it, as may uphold the Riches and Glory of it.

THE

REASONS

OF THE

DECAY

OF THE

Englifh-Trade.

PART. I.

Definitions.

WHat is Trade ?

Def. 1. Trade is an Art of Getting, Preparing, and Exchanging things Commodious for Humane Neceffities and Convenience.

Annot. So as Trade happens three ways. 1. By acquiring, or getting things commodious, which are called Growths. 2ly, By Preparing them, which are called Manufactures. 3ly, By Exchanging thefe Growths and Manufactures for Mony or other Growths and Manufactures.

And Trade is twofold, *viz.* Native, and Forein. 1, Native when the Growths or Manufactures are got, Prepared, and Exchanged upon the place. 2ly, Forein, when Growths and Manufactures are exchanged in Forein Places.

What

What is Mony?

2. Mony, is the Standard by which all things in Trade are valued.

What is Navigation?

3. Navigation is an Art of Conveying things upon the Body of the Waters from one place to another.

Who are the Dutch, intended in this Discourse?

4. Those who are subject to the States of the *United Netherlands.*

Who are the English?

5. Those who are born in Subjection to the Crown of England.

Who is a Dutch *Merchant?*

6. One who Trades under the Protection of the States of the *United Netherlands.*

Who is an English *Merchant?*

7. One who Trades under the Protection of the *English,* and born in Subjection to its Crown.

Who are the Dutch States?

8. They who govern Trade in the *United Netherlands,* and all places subject to them.

Who are the Council of State in England?

9. They are those Persons with whom the King pleases to Advise and Consult in State Affairs, where no Provision is made by Municipal Laws.

What are Corporations in Trade?

10. They are men, who in Trades where they are incorporated by Civil Power, exercise those Trades excluding all others.

Memorand. It is lawful to assume all things and places in Trade, under those names, by which they are usually called.

Petitions.

Pet. 1. The *Dutch* freely entertain men of all Nations in Trade, and grant them equal Priviledges with the Natural *Dutch.*

Pet. 2. The *English* Nation consumes all the Commodities of *France* imported into it.

Pet. 3. The *French* Commodities Imported into *England* do Exceed in Value the *Englifh* Commodities Exported into *France.*

Annot. Mr. *Fortrey*, a Gentleman of the Kings Privy Chamber, in his Treatife of *England's Intereft and Improvement*, pag.22, fays, That the excefs is above 1,600,000 *l.* a year, which did appear to the now King of *France* upon a defign he had to forbid Trade between *England* and *France*; and gives the Particulars, *pag.* 22, 23, 24. whereupon the King of *France* finding how much it would prove to his lofs, to forbid the Trade, laid it by, but raifed the Cuftom of fome of our *Englifh* Commodities, whereby the vent of them is much hindred.

Pet. 4. *England*, before it had the acceffion of our *American* Plantations, wanted men to Improve the Growths and Manufactures of it; and alfo the Fifhing Trade.

Annot. Sir *Walter Rawleigh* takes notice in his obfervations upon Trade, which he dedicated to King *James*, that this Kingdom, in 55 years loft above 25 Millions of Pounds, befides other incredible advantages, which would have accrued to this Kingdom in Strength and Trade by the *Dutch* Dreffing and Dying our White Clothes. I will not difpute, whether it had been good policy to have reftrained the Exportation of our White and Undreft Clothes: I only affirm that *England* could have better and cheaper Maintained and Imployed thofe men in Dreffing and Dying them, than *Holland* and *Amfterdam*, having no excife upon our Commodities, and Fullers Earth better and cheaper than in the United *Netherlands*. Befides *England* could then better and cheaper have maintained all thofe men, who in the United *Netherlands* fo much defired our Wooll, Lead, and Tin, in their Manufactures.

Sir *Walter Rawleigh* further takes notice that in four Towns in the Eaft Countries, whithin the *Sound*, *Queenfborough*, *Elbing*, *Statten*, and *Dantzick*, were yearly vented, between 30 and 40000 laft of Herring by the *Dutch*, at 15 or 16 *l.* the laft, which amounts to 620000 *l.* and by us none.

To

To *Denmark*, *Sweden*, *Lifeland*, *Rivel*, *Narue*, and other Ports within the *Sound*, there are Carried and vented by the *Dutch* above 10000 Laſt of *Herrings* at above 15 or 16 *l.* the Laſt, which amounts to about 170000 *l.*

Into *Ruſſia* the *Dutch* ſent about 1500 Laſt of Herrings, ſold at 30 *s.* the Barrel, which amounted to 27000 *l.* and we about 20 or 30 : I am ſure we ſend none now.

To *Stoad* , *Hamborough*, *Bream*, *Embden* upon the River *Elb*, *Weaſer*, and *Embs*, were carryed and vented of Fiſh and Herring 6000 Laſt, which at 15 or 16 *l.* by the Laſt amounted to 100000 *l.* by us none.

To *Clevleand*, *Gulickland*, and to *Germany* up the *Rhine* and *Maine*, were vented by the *Dutch* 2200 Laſt of Fiſh and Herring ſold at 20 *l.* the Laſt, which comes to 44000 *l.* by us none.

Up the River *Maze*, *Leigh*, *Maſtrick*, *Vendlow*, *Zutphen*, *Davinter*, *Campen*, *Swoll*, and all over *Lukeland*, is carried and vented 7000 Laſt of Herring by the *Dutch* at 140000 *l.* by us none.

To *Roan* were carried 5000 Laſt of Herring by the *Dutch*, and ſold at 20 *l.* the Laſt, which came to 100000 *l.* by us not 100 Laſt.

To *Gelderland*, *Artois*, *Henalt*, *Brabant*, *Flanders*, were carried between 8 and 9000 ſold at 18 *l.* the Laſt, which came to 171000 *l.* by us none.

Sir *Walter Rawleigh* left out *Spain*, and *France*, except *Roan*, and the *Dutch* Trade of Fiſh into the *Streights*, and what they conſumed among themſelves, which Queſtionleſs was and is now very conſiderable ; yet were all theſe Fiſh caught upon our Coaſt, and no queſtion, if we had, had the Hands, we might much better and cheaper have maintained them, and caught, and cured them, having many more, and much better and more convenient Ports than they.

Pet. 5. Mony is a convenient mean to improve Trade.

Pet. 6. Forein Trade is the only mean to Inrich this Kingdom.

Pet. 7. Multitude, and Concourſe of People, Advance Trade.   *Pet.* 8,

Pet. 8. Scarcity of People Diminifh Trade.

Pet. 9. The Law againft Naturalization permits no man of any other Nation to have equal Freedom and Priviledge in Trade, with the natural *Englifh.*

Pet. 10. The Law of Navigation Intituled, *Shipping and Navigation Encouraged,* made 12. *Car.* 2. 18. and continued, 13. *Car.* 2. 12. reftreins the *Englifh* in Navigation to Ships *Englifh* built, and to be failed by $\frac{3}{4}$ *Englifh* ; and Forein Commodities to be Imported by *Englifh* in Shipping fo built and failed, and to the Natives of the Place.

Pet. 11. The rents of Lands are valuable, as the Trade of the Place is.

Pet. 12. Stock is a convenient mean to advance Trade.

Pet. 13. Men are neceffary to improve Trade.

Pet. 14. Timber is a neceffary mean to build Ships.

Pet. 15. Ships are neceffary means in Navigation.

Pet. 16. The Timber of *England* was wanting even before the Act of Navigation, made 12. *Car.* 2. 18. and confirmed 13 *Car.* 2. 14. this appears by the Acts of 35. *H.* 8. 17. and 35. *El.* 11.

Pet. 17. The means ordained by the 1. *Eliz.* 13. and 35. *El.* 11. to fupply the Timber of *England* before wanting and decaied is interrupted by the Act of Navigation.

Pet. 18. Before the Act of Navigation, we wanted Shipping : this appears by the title of the Act, which is an Act for the encouraging and encreafe of Shipping and Navigation; for if we had not wanted Shipping, the encouraging and encreafing thereof, had been vain and fuperfluous.

Pet. 19. The lofs and decay of the Ships of *England* muft not in Navigation be fupplied by acquiring any Forein built Ships ; for by the Act of Navigation, if any *Englifh* man Trades in any Forein built Ship to any of our Plantations, or to any Port of *England,* or *Ireland,* it is Forfeit, Ship, Goods, Guns, Tackle, and Ammunition.

Pet. 20. Navigation is the only mean of vending our Growths and Manifactures, in Forein Trade unlefs it be into *Scotland.*

P4.

Pet. 21. The Act against the Importation of *Irish* Cattel made, 18. and 20. *Car.* 2. *cap.* 1. hath abated the Trade of *England*; with *Ireland* for Beer, Hops, and Bills of Exchange, for Money, all forts of Hats, and Stockings, Cloth, and Stuffs of all forts, Victualing Ships of all, as well Forein as *English*. &c.

Pet. 22. All the Canary Wines Imported into *England* are confumed in it.

Pet. 23. The Canary Wines Imported do exceed in value the *English* Commodities Exported into the Canaries. I cannot exactly compute the excefs; but have it from good hands, that the Canary Wines yearly Imported are about 13000 Pipes, which are valued at 20 *l.* the Pipe, which amounts to 200000 *l.* yearly; and that our Commodities Exported do not neer amount to ⅓ fo much in value : before we did exceed fo much in drinking them, we Imported them at 10 *l.* the Pipe, and Traded to the Canaries only upon the account of our Commodities in Barter for the Wines.

Actions or Common Notions.

1. Where the means of Improving any bufinefs are wanting, that bufinefs will be fo much diminifhed, as the means by which it might have been fupplied are diverted.

2. Where any thing is wanting and decaied, that thing will be fo much diminifhed, as the means of fupplying it are interrupted.

3. If the means of doing any thing be wanting, that thing will be fo much hindred, as the means are diminifhed.

4. The doing of things will be fo much hindred, as the means of doing them are hindred.

5. Every thing will be fo much diminifhed, as is abated of it.

6. Any bufinefs will be fo much hindred, by how much the means of improving it are excluded.

7. Where the confumption of things imported, does exceed in value the things Exported, the lofs will be as the excefs is.

Prop. 1. *Theorems.* 1.

The Trade of *England,* and the Fishing Trade, are so much diminished, by how much they might have been supplied by those men who are diverted in our *American* Plantations,

Subjects. The Trades of *England,* and the Fishing Trade.

Question. Whether they be so much diminished by how much they might have been supplyed? *&c.* I say they are.

Ax. 1. For where the means of improving any business are wanting, that business will be so much diminished, by how much the means, by which it might have been supplied, are diverted.

Pet. 24. But men are necessary to improve Trade.

Pet. 25. And before we had our *American* Plantations, we wanted men to improve the Trade of *England,* and the Fishing Trade.

Therefore the Trade of *England,* and the Fishing Trade, are so much diminished, by how much they might have been supplyed, by those men who are diverted in our *American* Plantations. Which was to be demonstrated.

Corollary. 1.

By the same reason the Trade of *England,* and the Fishing Trade, are so much more diminished, by how many men are diverted from supplying them in Repeopling *Ireland,* since the Late Massacre and War there.

Corollary. 2.

By the same reason the Trade of *England,* and the Fishing Trade are yet so much more diminished, by so many men, as extraordinarily died in the late great Plague, 1665.

Annotations

Annotations upon this Proposition and the two Corrollaries.

Before we had our *American* Plantations, the Coasts of
England were in a convenient manner Planted; and the
Multitudes of Inhabitants in *England* such, that in the 2.
and 3. *Ph.* and *Mary* 3. the Parliament taking notice that
a great number of persons within the Realm, had laid
their Lands, Farmes, and Pastures, to Feeding of Sheep,
Oxen, Runts, Schrubbes, Steers, and Heifers, and such like
Cattel, having no regard to breed and rear up young
Beasts and Cattel, whereby was grown great scarcity of
Cattel, and necessary victual for sustenance of divers sorts
of People within this Realm, and more like to be if speedy
remedy were not provided, therefore several provisions
were made for breeding and rearing of Cattel.

Experience had made tryal and proof of the goodness,
of this Law, to be very beneficial and profitable to this
Realm; and therefore in the 13. *El.* 25. it was made per-
petual; and as a very profitable Law the Act of 7. *Jac.* 8.
makes it to extend to grounds which were since inclosed or
hereafter should be inclosed.

Before the *Dutch* became *States*, or when at least they
were but *The Poor Distressed States*, besides our staple at
Antwerp we had the sole Trade into *Muscovy*, *Turkey*,
and up the *Elb* whereby *Germany*, *Denmarks*, *Jutland*, *Hol-
stein*, &c. were supplyed with our Cloth and Wollen Manufactures. We did moreover supply *Muscovy* with Fish,
and in a considerable measure, *France*, *Spain*, *Italy*, and
several parts of the World within the *Streights*.

And for the further encouragement of the Fishing
Trade, and for the preservation of the breeding of Cattel;
In the 5. *Eliz.* 5. It was ordained that *Wednesday*, as well
as *Friday*, and *Saturday*, should be observed as a Fish day
within this Realm, upon pain that every person offending,
should for every time he or they should offend, forfeit
3 *l.* or suffer three Months Imprisonment without Bail or
Mainprize, and every person, who was knowing thereof,
and

and concealed it, for every such offence should forfeit forty shillings, which Act yet continues in force, but only the Penalty of eating Flesh upon Fridaies, Saturdaies, and Wednesdaies is reduced by the 35 *Eliz.* 7 to twenty shillings, and the concealing of it by any Person, knowing it, to ten shillings.

Consequences of this Proposition and the two Corollaries.

After our *American* Plantations became peopled by us, the *Dutch* began to partake with us in the *Turky* and *Muscovy* Trades; our Staple at *Antwerp* diminished in a very great measure, to intend the Trades to our Plantations, we neglected the Fishing Trade, whereby (except the Trade of red Herrings, which cannot be cured by the *Dutch*) the *Dutch* in a manner became solely in a short time possessed of it, and thereby have acquired this incomparable advantage above us in the Trade of our Plantations; that as we imploy only our ablest men in trading to them, who in the diversity of Clime and Diet are very subject to Diseases and Mortality; and leave the impotent Women and Children at home without imploiment; they imploy three times more men in the Fishing trade, and four times more to the benefit of their State, and also all manner of impotent People, Women, and Children; and have this advantage above us in time of War as well as Peace, that all hands imployed in the Fishing Trade are at home, and serviceable when they are at War; whereas the Inhabitants in our Plantations are of no use or benefit to us in War, which was very apparent in our late War with them.

The Coast of *England* (which should be the Glory, Strength, and Ornament of an Island) in peopling of them, and loss of the Fishing Trade, soon became decaid; nor was there, or now is there, as the case stands, any possible relief herein; for necessarily so much as is taken from any thing, so much less will be left; and the law against Naturalization debarring a future supply, the Addition of our Miseries in the Massacre of *Ireland* and the late great Plague, the supp'ying *Ireland* hath
not

not only rendred the Coaſt deſolate; but the Country too becomes thin and uninhabited: From whence notwithſtanding we obſerve none of the Fiſh-daies (which were above half the year)enjoyned by the 5 *Eliz.* 5. nor the ſeveral Laws made by King *Philip* and *Mary*, Queen *Elizabeth*, and King *James*, for breeding of Cattel, and have excluded the Kingdom of *Ireland* from trading with us in Cattel, yet our Markets are plentifully enough ſupplied with them; nay, the Graziers are ſo overſtocked, that they want Markets for them. This Miſchief moreover attends this Nation, That as Neceſſity is the Mother of Ingenuity, ſo the Law againſt Naturalization debarrs all Ingenuous men to plant with us; and *Ireland* and our Plantations are open Gates, for all neceſſitous and ingenuous men to run out from us, and ſettle in them; where, but eſpecially in *Ireland*, for little they may lead an idle and lazy life.

In this condition I leave to thee, Reader, to judg, whether it will not be yet ſo much more pernicious to the Trade of this Nation to endeavour a further diſcovery of new Plantations; and that if the Project of Peopling *Carolina* from the Reſidue of the men we have left in *England*, if it ſucceeds, will not ſo much more enfeeble this Nation, and reduce the Trade thereof to ſo much a leſs proportion by how many men ſhall be withdrawn from it?

We ſee in ſome ſort the Influence the Law againſt Naturalization hath upon our Trade: Let us conſider the influence it hath upon the Strength and Welfare of it, now we have peopled our Plantations, and repeopled *Ireland*, ſince the late War and Maſſacre there, and compare it with the Kingdom of *Spain*.

Spain in old time, if Credit may be given to *Livy* and *Plutarch*, was the moſt warlike, and continued longeſt and ſharpeſt Wars againſt the *Romans*, though it were ſubject to many little Kings; and it is ſcarce credible, with what huge Armies they did maintain it. And as in old times, ſo in this later Age, when *Spain* was divided into the Kingdoms of *Caſtile* and *Leon, Arragon, Portugal, Navarr,* and *Granado*, in the Reigns of *Fernando* and *Iſabella,*
the

the War againſt the *Moors* was proſecuted purely by the Kingdom of *Caſtile* and *Leon* ; for *Arragon* refuſed to contribute to it, and *Navarr* and *Portugal* ſtood neuters, and were not concerned in it. Yet it is admirable to read with what huge Armies for 10 years together (for ſo long the War laſted) *Fernand* and *Iſabella* continued thoſe wars ; and it was in their Reigns, that *Columbus* made his Diſcovery and Attempts upon the *Weſt-Indies* : whereas all the *Spains* now are united (except *Portugal*) under one Monarchy, and have moreover, for ought is known, acceſſion of greater Dominions than any Kingdoms of the Weſtern or perhaps of the Eaſtern World, it is become ſo weak and feeble, as it is a Queſtion whether it be in the power of *Chriſtendom* to ſupport it againſt the power of *France* ; and the King of *Spain*, though Lord of all the Treaſure of the *Weſt-Indies*, of the greateſt and richeſt is fallen to be the pooreſt and weakeſt Prince of *Chriſtendom* : nor can any other reaſon be given hereof (at leaſt that I underſtand) but removing the *Moors* out of *Granado*, the tranſporting ſo many *Spaniards* into the *Weſt-Indies*, and the Inquiſition which barrs out any future Supply.

Let us take notice of the weakneſs of *Spain*, both at home and in his *Weſt-Indies*. In ſome particulars, when *Portugal* made Defection from the Crown of *Spain* ; *Spain* without any ſucceſs for neer 20 years maintained War againſt it, chiefly by Souldiers brought out of *Milan*, *Naples*, *Sicily*, and ſuch Forces as it hired out of *Germany* and *Switzerland* ; (for few could be raiſed out of *Spain*) But this proving inſucceſsful, truſting to the *Gallick* faith in the Treaty at *Bayonne*, 1659, the King of *Spain* brought the Marqueſs *Caracen*, and the greateſt part of the Army in the *Netherlands*, to continue the Wars againſt *Portugal* ; but this Army being broken by the joint force of the *Engliſh*, *French* and *Portuguez*, *Spain* was ever after forced to continue upon a defenſive poſture, until it was neceſſitated to ſeek a peace by the loſs of the Kingdom of *Portugal* ; and what the conſequences of the loſs of the Army under the Marqueſs of *Caracen* have been to the *Spaniſh Netherlands* in the
year

year, 1667, is underſtood very well by the *Engliſh*, *Dutch*, and *Switz*, and the conſeqnences yet further feared by them.

And as the weakneſs of *Spain* is ſuch at home, ſo it is more in his *Indies*, from whence his Wealth and Riches flow, and for ought is known they are greater than any Prince in the World hath; yet being but thinly planted, how eaſily do they every year receive the impulſion, devaſtation and plunder of a few *Jamaican* Capers?

But ſure it were worthy conſideration how to prevent this for the future: for if the vaſt exhauſting of the Treaſure of the *Engliſh* and *Dutch* in their *French*, *Eaſt-Indy*, *Turky* and other Eaſtern Trades, were not ſupplied out of the *Spaniſh Weſt-Indies*, theſe Trades muſt either be diſcontinued, or theſe Weſtern parts of the World, in a ſhort time, would be utterly impoveriſhed by them: ſo as it is evident both *Engliſh* and *Dutch* muſt neceſſarily ſuffer ſo much, by how much theſe *Jamaicans* impoveriſh, or interrupt the King of *Spain* or his Subjects in the returns of his Plate-Fleets, and I may ſafely ſay the *Engliſh* Nation looſes ten times more than the *Jamaicans* get by every Quickſilver Ship they take from the King of *Spain* or his Subjects.

The State of *England* compar'd with that of *Spain*.

Let us compare the State of *England* with that of *Spain*, and ſee if from not unlike cauſes it does not neceſſarily degenerate into the Condition of it. Firſt, *Ireland* and our Plantations, do in proportion to *England* more exhauſt it of men, than the *Weſt-Indles* do *Spain*; and if no proviſion be made will in leſs time, than ſince the *Weſt-Indies* came to be ſubject to the Crown of *Spain*, leave it leſs peopled. Secondly, The Maſſacre in *Ireland*, wherein is ſaid 300000 Proteſtants were murthered, and probably as many of the Rebels ſuffered, the late Plague wherein neer 200000 perſons died, and our late Civil and Forein Wars do more than equalize the tranſplanting the *Moors* out of *Granade*; and Laſtly, the Law againſt Naturalization, is a greater Bar to a future Supply in *England*, than the Inquiſition is in *Spain*.

We

We have compared the Condition of *England* and *Spain*, now I will inſtance wherein the Condition of *England* is worſe by our Plantations, than *Spain* is by theirs. Firſt, in that the Crown of *Spain* in the *Weſt-Indies* acquires new Subjects; whereas we in our Plantations, wholly people them from our ſelves : And the King of *Spain* being head of the Houſe of *Auſtria*, beſides the ſupplies, which he draws out of *Milan, Naples, Sicily,* and *Switzerland,* hath upon all occaſions large ſupplies of men out of *Germany.*

Before we had our Plantations, *England*, when it was not troubled with Civil Wars, did uſually in their offenſive Wars prevail againſt *France* and *Scotland.* I cannot tell whether the Coaſts of *England* be better planted than the Coaſts of the King of *Spain's Weſt-Indies* : I am ſure the *French* King and *Dutch* are more able to attempt the invading of them, than the *Jamaicans* thoſe of the *Weſt-Indies.*

By this Law againſt Naturalization we bid defiance to all the World to continue our Adverſaries, and deny the Aſſiſtance of all Proſelytes, who otherwiſe might be of us, and aſſiſt us. Whereas the Prudence and Practice of the *Romans* and greateſt and wiſeſt Princes and Potentates of the World, for which they have been and now are celebrated famous, have proceeded otherwiſe : and this may be more fully underſtood in Sir *Walter Rawleigh's Safety and Defence of People,* &c. And God himſelf would not permit the *Jews* to continue in the Land he had given them, unleſs they did not oppreſs the Stranger. *Jer.* 7. 6, 7.

1. As the Law of Naturalization debarrs us of any future Supply for all the Strength and Trade, which this Nation loſes in peopling our Plantations, and repeopling *Ireland* ; ſo it was the Reaſon that before we had our Plantations, this Nation loſt to the *Dutch* above 48000 pounds *per An.* in dying and dreſſing our Manufactures ; and above 1645000 pounds *per An.* in the Fiſhing Trade ; for this Nation could have better and by half cheaper have maintained the Managers, if this Law had permitted.

2. This

2. This Law is the Reafon that thofe Multitudes of hands which are imployed abroad in our Woollen Manufactures, are not imployed here. So that by the feverity of many Laws againſt the Exportation of Wool, we reſtrain our Wool from forein Trade, and by this Law we exclude the World from working it here; whereby our Wool becomes a drug and of no eſteem, being neither well wrought at home, and not permitted in forein Trade.

3. This Law is the Reafon that in our Tin and Lead we are the only Drudges to work it out of the Mines, whilſt all parts of the World but our felves, improve Trade, and grow rich by Manufactures thereon.

Corollary. 3.

By the fame Reafon the Trade of *England*, and the Fiſhing Trade are fo much more diminiſhed by how much they might be fupplied by thofe hands, and fo much Money as is diverted from them in relief of idle perfons by the Statute of the 43 of *Eliz.* intit. *Who ſhall be Overfeers for the Poor, their Office, Duty, and Accounts.*

Annotations.

Reader, That the Mifchiefs and Inconveniences which have enfued this Law may better appear, take with thee thefe Confiderations. Firſt, That God hath made Man to eat his bread in the cares of Mind, and fweat of his brows; that man therefore who neither cares nor labours, hath no reafon to expect that he ſhall have any thing to care for. Secondly, Confider that the Nation was much more inhabited when this Law was made, than now. From hence then, Reader, take a Profpect of the Inconveniences, which have enfued this Law.

1. That where pure Neceffity does not require, it inverts the end which God hath by Nature made; *viz.* That where Man does not care for and govern, he ſhould eat his bread by Labour and Induſtry.

2. That

2. That notwithstanding our great loss and want of men, for the reasons beforesaid, these idle persons provided for by this Act, are so more a loss to the Nation than if they had never been, by how much the Nation loses in maintaining, and providing for them: and this is encreased to such a height that notwithstanding the want of men, more now than when this Law was made, yet the charge of maintaining poor people in very many Places is 6, 7, 8, 9 fold more than before: and what the further consequences hereof will be, if not prevented, is most worthy the consideration of the Parliament.

3. It is a discouragement to all industrious and labouring people, when lazy and idle people shall be maintained in their idleness from the fruits of their Labour and Industry.

4. It encourages wilful and evil disposed persons to impose what wages they please upon their labours; and herein they are so refractory to Reason and the benefit of the Nation, that when Corn and Provisions are cheap, they will not work for less wages than when they were dearer, so as it often happens that one days indifferent labour, shall maintain these persons three or four days after in Idleness; which if this Law had not been, might have been for a reserve to support themselves and families in adversity and sickness.

5. As sundry Laws provided against wandring Beggers and Vagabonds, so this Law provides for, and relieves stationary Beggers.

6. This Law is the principal, if not the only reason of the excessive wages of servants as well as labourers; in making Provision for such, who will neither serve, nor labour.

7. From this Law therefore it is principally (and for the want of good education of the governing part of the Trade of the Nation, of which we shall treat hereafter) that as Mr. *Mun* observes in his excellent treatise of *England's Treasure by Forein Trade,* cap. 19. that the *English* Nation is reproached commonly among strangers for the multitudes of

of People which in *England* Cheat, Roar, Rob, Hang, Beg, Cant, Pine and Perifh; which otherwife might help to encreafe and maintain the Wealth and ftrength of thefe Kingdomes, efpecially by Sea, for our own fafety and terrour of our enemies.

8. The charity which might be imployed in the refeife of truely impotent and aged people is heerby abated and diminifhed.

Corollary. 4.

By the fame reafon the Trade of *England* and the Fifhing Trade are fo much more diminifhed, by how much they might be fupplyed by thofe lazy and idle perfons, who are diverted from them, by living upon Wafts, Commons, Chafes and Forefts.

Annotations.

So as this difference is between thefe perfons, and thofe maintained by the 43. *El.* 2. that as thofe are maintained by the lofs of the Nation; fo thefe are maintained to no benefit of it: but are dangerous as well to the Nation, as Government of it. This appeas by the Riots and Tumults, which they make upon all Endeavours of Improvments, notwithftanding compenfations are made double and treble to the value of what they reaped thereby. The number therefore of thefe kind of perfons encreafing, which daily does, as well by a fucceffion of thofe who are born upon fuch places, as otherwife, and being at liberty to work or not, the Government will be fo much more endangered by how much they are encreafed; and fo much more by how much lefs thefe Commons, Chafes, Wafts, and Forefts can maintain them; to fupply which, breaking Hedges, cutting Woods, and ftealing Fowl, *&c.* are the ufual means by which they make up their living.

How advantageous it would be to the Trade of the Nation, if all thefe idle hands were imployed in it; and how great a Reuenue might be raifed out of thefe Wafts,

if

if they were improved and imployed in Trade, and binding out Prentices, and in defraying Publique charges, were moſt worthy Conſideration of the Parliament.

Corollary. 5.

By the ſame reaſon, the Trade of *England,* and the Fiſhing Trade are ſo much more diminiſhed, by how much they might be ſupplyed by thoſe perſons, who are diverted form them in being hanged.

Apology.

I do not diſpute the Authority of any Law in this Corollary, or in any Corollary or Propoſition in this diſcourſe; I only contend that the ends deſigned by Legiſlators, are not always attained; and therefore Anciently our Anceſtors were ſo careful of preparing Laws, that they uſually made them not longer lived than the end of the next Seſſion of Parliament; ſo that, if the end deſigned by them were not attained, the Laws themſelves ſhould expire. The end of puniſhing Malefactors is twofold, *viz.* to deter others from Committing Crimes, and for the Offender to make Reſtitution ſo far as he is able. But I do not underſtand that the end of puniſhment is to deſtroy, where murder or a higher Crime is not the offence. Nor is Hanging, which is tranſient, ſo Permanent a Terror to offendors, as a conſtant inflicting extraordinary duties upon Offendors, whereby they might, or in a great meaſure might expiate their Crimes by ſatisfying the perſons Offended. Nothing in nature but by ſome means or other might be made beneficial, ſure therefore much more man; nor does man diſtroy in any thing elſe, but on the life of Man, where any other means can be found to preſerve, and the end, in making reſtitution, is holy loſt.

Corollary. 6 §.

Corollary. 6.

By the fame reafon, the Trade of *England*, and the Fifhing Trade, are yet fo much more diminifhed, by how much they might be fupplyed by thofe men, who are diverted from them, in being imprifoned for debt.

Annotations.

Herein moreover is the end defigned in Punifhing Offendors inverted, for in being committed prifoners, the means which is thereby fpent in paying Fees to Jaylors, is inverted from that end to which it might have been imployed towards the Payment of his Debts; and the perfons of the Prifoners made ufelefs any ways by labour or induftry to contribute to the fatisfaction thereof.

Corollary. 7.

By the fame reafon the Trade of *Englaud*, and Fifhing Trade are fo much diminifhed, by how much mony and fo many men as are diverted from fupplying them in buying and morgaging Land.

Pet. 5. For mony is a convenient mean to improve Trade.

Annotations upon this Corollary.

Before we contended that the Law againft Naturalization, makes the Kingdom weak and unable to improve the Trade therof; in this Corollary we complain of a practice againft Law and Confcience too. For by the Statute of *Weftminfter*, 2. made the 13. *Edw.* 1. c. 4. it was provided that Eftates in Tail fhould remain to the Donee, and his Heirs according to the form of the gift of the Donor, and for want of iffue of the Donee, to revert to the Donor and his Heirs: And that Fines levied
upon

upon fuch claimes be void. Yet by what practice or ufage
Fines come to Barr Heirs in Tail; and recovery of thofe
in remainder I cannot tell. I am fure the Will of the
Donor, (which in Confcience ought religioufly to be obferved,) is hereby violated: And all that mony which is
expended in Buying and Morgaging fuch Lands, is diverted
from the good ufe by which it might be imployed in
Trade; befides the multitudes of mifchiefs, which arife
in vexatious Suits between Vendor and Vendee, Morga-
ger and Morgagee, to the utter undoing one another;
whereby multitudes of Solicitors, Bankers, Ufurers, and
Scriveners, (who no ways advance the Trade of the Nation) become vaftly rich, whileft the Trade of the Nation
hereby becomes ftarved and neglected, and by confequence
the Nation fo much poorer. By reafon hereof the Stock
of this Nation fuppofing it double to the *Dutch* ; yet do
I not believe one fixt part fo much is imploied by us in
Trades beneficial to the Nation, as by them ; and I wifh
this Quere were determined, Whether from this caufe
the Bankers and Scriveners of *London* cannot raife more
Money, in one week, than the Parliament of *England* can in
two years?

*How many ways this Kingdom might be enriched, and the
Trade thereof encreafed, if the Statute of* Weftminfter. 2.
made 13. Edw. 1. c. 1. *were obferved.*

1. The Will of the Donor (which by all Laws of Religion and Gratitude ought religioufly to be obferved)
would not be violated, for which we may juftly fear the
Judgments and Vengeance of God.

2. The vaft and wild Prodigality of vain men and women, would be reftrained within the bounds of their
Eftates: And the impoverifhment, which they bring
upon the Kingdom by their Pride, Vanity and Luxury,
in a very great meafure would be abated.

3. The Families of the Nobility and Gentry, would
hereby be preferved and continued.

4. The multitudes of Solicitors, Bankers, Scriveners
and

ard usurers, who now (warm more than ever, and devour all the good of the Nation, but no ways do any good to it, would diminish, and these very men be necessitated, to seek some better means of substistence, whereby the Kingdom might receive benefit, now we so much want hands to advance the Trade of the Nation.

5. The Supernumerary Pages, Lacquies, and Waiting Women, who are Moths to fret and consume their Masters and Ladies Estates, might be imploied in ways beneficial to the Kingdom.

6. The Stock of the Nation to be imploied in beneficial Trades would be tenfold more imploied in them.

7. The Riches acquired by Trade; would continually be imploied in it, as well as in the *United Netherlands*.

8. The Interest of Mony without a Law, would fall to be as low, as in the *United Netherlands*.

9. Men would be more intent to improve their Estates, when they know what they must betake themselves to; and may more securely follow their business, than when they are engaged in Law Suits about Morgages and Titles of Land.

Reader thou mayst add many more, but if any man shall give me one for not observing this Law, I will give him all my nine.

Proposition. 2. *Theorem.* 2.

The Timber of *England* is diminished, and is in danger to be destroyed, by the Act of the 12. *Car.* 2. 18. and confirmed 13. *Car.* 2. 18. Entituled *An Act for Encouraging and encrease of Shipping and Navigation*; and commonly called *the Act of Navigation.*

Subject, Is the Timber of *England.*

Question. *Whether it be diminished by the Act of Navigation?* I say it is.

Ax. 2. For where any thing is wanting and decayed, that thing will be more diminished, if the means of supplying it be interrupted.

Pet. 4.

Pet. 4. But the Timber of *England* was wanting and decayed before the Act of Navigation.

Pet. 17. And the means of supplying the Timber of *England*, is interrupted by the Act of Navigation.

Therefore the Timber of *England*, is diminished by the Act of Navigation. Which was to be demonstrated.

Annotations upon this Proposition.

It is now above 120 years since the making of the Act of 35. of *H.* 8. 17. when without all question the Timber of *England*, was above five times more than now it is; yet notwithstanding the heat and distemper of those times, so vigilant were our Ancestors in the preservation of the Timber of this Nation, (the best For Shipping in the world) that though they did not foresee all ways for preserving and encreasing it ; yet they saw that the great decay of it, was universally such in *England*, that unless speedy remedy in that behalf were provided, great and manifest likelyhood of scarcity, and lack of Timber for building, making, repairing, and maintaining Houses and Ships would be ; for prevention whereof several provisions were made; but never put (or at least not in my memory) in execution. Which is the fate in many of the Laws of these times. *Queen Elizabeth,* a Lady of incomparable Prudence and Foresight, and more jealous of the Honour and Safety of this Nation, than any of her Ancestors or predecessors) as one of her chiefest cares, in the first year of her Reign, for the Preservation of the Timber of *England,* gave free liberty to all men, as well Subjects as Strangers, freely to Import Masts and Raff. Notwithstanding this provision, this vigilant Queen, taking notice of the great decay of Timber occasioned by converting the same into cloven board, did, in the 35. of her Reign, *cap.* 11. Ordain, that every stranger which should ship, carry, or Transport Bere, or Fish (except Herrings) in Cask, should before such Transportation ; and every Subject which should Transport Beer or Fish before, or within four months after,

for

for every six tuns of Beer or Fish, should import from parts beyond the Seas, 200 of clapboard fit to make Cask to contain three foot and two inches in length at least, upon penalty of forfeiture of such Fish, Beer, and Cask. Yet though both these laws stand now in force, and the good and safety of the Nation be so much concerned in them; the Act of Navigation makes it forfeiture of Ship, Goods and Guns to import any Raff, Masts, Timber, or Clapboard, unless by *English* ships (though the *English* since the Rumps first institution of the Law have not built one ship for this Trade, nor ever will so long as it stands in force) and sayled by ¾ *English*, and the Natives of the place, whether the Natives have ships or not. So that if an *English* man, *Dutch* man, *Hamburger*, or any Easterling Trade for beer or fish, and doe not import the clapboard prescribed by the 35 *Eliz.* 11. the goods and cask are forfeit: But if they do import clapboard, the ship and goods and guns are forfeit by the Act of Navigation.

I have often heard my Father complain of the vast destruction of our Timber by converting the same into Clapboard, whereby all the best of our Timber is consumed; for when any Oak will rend, or so far as the ground end will rend, Rift bearing about a third penny more price then if it were sawn into planck, the converter intending his profit converts it into Rift ; and that if he could ever see a Parliament wherein he could ever hope to do any good, he would bring in a Bill to prevent the destruction of our Timber hereby.

Old *Oliver* entertain'd this Law but coldly, but however he were otherwise more careful of his own Interest than of the Nations ; yet he permitted the *English* Merchants to trade in Forein Bottoms for Timber, whereby he was not only better and cheaper supplied than the Nation hath since been, but he enforced the King of *Denmarks* Subjects to sell their ships built for that Trade, and wherewith they used to impose what terms they pleased upon the *English*, being better and cheaper supplyed than they could.

Consequences

Confequences of this Propofition.

Befides the mifchiefs and inconveniences which have come upon this Nation by not obferving the Law made the 35 of *Eliz.* 11. thefe inconveniences have enfued the Act of Navigation, in reference to the Trade of Timber, which were proved before a Committee of the Houfe of Commons laft Seffion of Parliament.

1. Before the Rump made this Law, the Trade to *Norway* for Timber, was generally driven by the *Englifh* in barter of our growths and Manufactures ; whereas now it is driven in Dollars and the Treafure of the Nation; and thofe Growths and Manufactures of *England* which are exported into *Norway* are rarely exported but by *Norwegians.*

2. That the prizes of *Norway* timber were become near double.

3. That our own Timber was much wafted by reafon of the dearnefs of *Norway.*

4. That we had not built one fhip for that Trade fince the Law, nor could ever hope to do fo long as it ftood in force, becaufe a forein fhip may be built for half the price, and be more free for Trade ; whereas the *Norwegians* had doubled their fhipping ; and built them twice as bigg; and from 600 Mariners, encreafed them to 6000 ; whereby the *Englifh* in a fhort time muft neceffarily be excluded the Trade of *Norway,* unlefs he drive it by *Norwegians,* and in *Norway* bottoms.

5. That the *Englifh* are now almoft wholly laid afide; the Trade of *Norway* being generally driven in *Norway* bottoms and thofe fayled by *Norwegians.*

6. That the *Englifh* are wholly left to the King of *Denmarkes* difpofing, whenever he pleafes to impofe any further abufes upon them than were complained of; which were that the *Englifh* ever fince 1646. and by the treaty made with his Majefty 1660. paid ¾ of a Rixdollar *per Laft* for the growths of *Norway* (except the Town of *Bergen*) but fince the late War with them, they paid cuftome for Timber a
                                                            Rixdollar

Rixdollar and half *per Laſt*, for other growth, a Rixdollar, and ⅘, others 2 Rixdollars and ⅔, and others 3 Rixdollars, and in meaſuring the Laſtage, the ſame ſhips which before the War had their meaſures adjuſted were raiſed ſome 35 others 40 Laſts.

7. That it was the Intereſt of the King of *Denmark* to make the Trade of *Norway* inſupportable to the *Engliſh*, for thereby as the caſe ſtood his Subjects would monopolize the Trade, yet could no redreſs hereof be had, untill in the years 1667, 1668. his Majeſty permitted his Subjects to Trade in Forein Veſſels, and ſtrangers to import Timber; and this reduced the Exorbitant Impoſitions of the King of *Denmark* to the Treaty of 1660, or otherwiſe he would have undone his own Subjects in that Trade, as they were in the time of *Oliver*.

I inſiſt more particularly hereon, becauſe that by the ſcarcity and waſte of our Timber by reaſon of this Law, and which muſt be in a vaſt meaſure increaſed in rebuilding the City of *London*, the *French* and *Dane* will have in their own Dominions, and the *Dutch* may have down the *Rhine*, *Maze*, and *Scheld* out of *Germany*, *Liege*, and *Lorrain*, ſuch Quantities of Timber, as between any of them and us will be no proportion; and what the fatal conſequence hereof will be to this Nation, if no care or proviſion be had, I almoſt tremble to conſider.

Propoſition, 3. Theorem, 3.

The Building Ships in *England* is hindred by the Act of Navigation.

Subject, is the Building Ships in *England*.

Queſt. *Whether it be diminiſhed by the Act of Navigation?* I ſay it is.

Ax. 3. For if the means of doing any thing be wanting, that thing will be ſo much hindred, as the means of ſupplying it are diminiſhed.

Pet. 16. But the Timber of *England* before the Act of Navigation was wanting for Building Ships in *England*.

Pet. 14.

Pet. 14. And Timber is a neceffary mean to build Ships.

Prop. 2. The Timber of *England* is diminifhed by the Act of Navigation.

Therefore the Building Ships in *England* is hindred by the Act of Navigation. Which was to be demonftrated.

Annotations upon this Propofition.

It is agreed upon by all men that the Timber of *England* is of all other the beft for Building Ships ; but then it muft be underftood, that like choice may be had in *England*, as in other places ; and fo long as we had as good choice in our *Englifh* Timber, as the *Dutch*, *Dane*, and *French*, we built better Men of War, and ftronger and more durable Merchants Ships, than any of them : But now all the choice Timber of *England* is wafted and confumed; the *Dutch*, *Dane*, and *French* have equal choice as before, it is much to be feared that for the future we fhall not long enjoy this Advantage, but not be able without exceffive charge to build fo good Ships as any of them.

Propofition 4. *Theorem* 4.

The Ships of *England* are diminifhed by the Act of Navigation?

Subject, is the Ships of *England*.

Queftion, *Whether they be diminifhed by the Act of Navigation?*

I fay they are.

Ax. 3. For where the doing things are hindred, and the lofs and decay of thofe things not otherwife fupplied, thefe things will be diminifhed.

Prop. 3. But the building Ships in *England* is hindred by the Act of Navigation.

Pet. 19. And the lofs and decay of Ships of *England* muft not be fupplied in acquiring any Forein Ships by the Act of Navigation.

Therefore

Therefore the Ships of *England* are diminished by the Act of Navigation. Which was to be demonstrated.

Annotation.

I do not understand how this Law makes good the title of it; For I am confident at this day is not one half of the Shipping in *England*, take prize ships into the reckoning, (which I guess to be above 4 times more than the *English* lost in both the late *Dutch* wars.) In *Ispwich* are somewhat above one third of what were, when the Rump instituted this Law ; At *Wood-bridg* not one third ; and at *Alborough*, *Dunwitch* , *Walders-wick* and sould not one fourth, as were before this Law. And I wish some man would take pains to make further inspecti-on herein to prove me mistaken.

Proposition 5. Theorem 5.

The Navigation of *England* is hindred by the Act of Navi-gation.

Subject, The Navigation of *England.*

Question , *Whether it be hindred by the Act of Naviga-tion ?*

I say it is.

Ax. 2. For the doing things will be so much hindred, as the necessary means of Doing them is Diminished.

Prop. 4. But the Ships of *England* are diminished by the Act of Navigation.

Pet. 3. And ships are necessary in Navigation.

Therefore the Navigation of *England* is hindred by the Act of Navigation. Which was to be demonstrated. So as we can neither build ships, nor can we buy;

Annotations.

Nor must any *English* man navigate any English built ship to trade to any part of *England* , *Ireland,* or any of our Plantations, unless she be sailed by ¾ *English* at least, under
on

no lefs penalty than lofs of Ship, Goods, Guns, Ammunition, and Tackle ; though it be evident the Coaſt of *England* be defolate and almoſt uninhabited : and the Country as well as Coaſt is fo thin of People, that it is not half peopled.   By the Act of 1 *Eliz.* 13. It was free for all men as well ſtrangers as Natives to import Pitch and Tar , which Law ſtands yet in force ; yet if by the Act of Navigation any *Engliſh* man, unleſs in *Engliſh* built ſhips, and failed by ¼ *Engliſh* import any ; or any ſtranger not Natives, whether the Natives have Ships or not, import any , the Ship Goods, Guns, Tackle and Ammunition are all forfeit.   So by the 1 *Eliz.* 13. All men might import hemp and cordage paying ſtrangers duties.   Now if any *Engliſh* ſhip import any hemp or cordage and be not failed by ¼ *Engliſh* at leaſt ſhe is forfeit *&c.* nor muſt any ſtranger not Native upon any leſs penalty : Yet it is evident that the Inhabitants of *Leifland*; from whence the beſt hemp (if not all) is to be had, trade not with us at all.

Confequenſies.

From whence it came to paſs that in two years after the Rump, making this Law, the building of ſhips became one third penny dearer ; and Sea-mens wages fo exceſſive that we have wholly loſt the Trades to *Muſcovy* and *Greenland* thereby : and from hence it is, that all Forein Commodities; imported into *England* (except in the *Turkey* Trade, and ſome Trifles from *Guiney* and the *Eaſt-Indies*) are conſumed in *England* ; whilſt thereby we give the *Dutch* and other Nations a power of driving the Trade of the World, where the Commodities are not *Engliſh* or ſubject to the Crown of *England.*

Propoſition 6. Theorem 6.

The Trade of *England* and of Fiſhing into Forein Parts is hindred by the Act of Navigation.

Subject,

Subject, The Trade of *England* and of Fishing into Forein parts.

Question, *Whether it be hindred by the Act of Navigation?* I fay it is.

Ax. 4. For the doing things will be hindred fo much, as the neceffary means of doing them are hindred.

Pet. 20. But Navigation is the only means of vending the Growths and Manufactures of *England*, and Fishing in Forein Trade, unlefs it be in *Scotland*.

Prop. 5. And the Navigation of *England* is hindred by the Act of Navigation.

Therefore the Trade of *England* and of Fishing into forein parts is hindred by it. Which was to be demonftrated.

Annotations.

Nor muft any Forein fhip or veffel trade to *England* with any forein Commodities, unlefs in fhips or veffels of that place or Country, and Navigated by the Mr. and ⅔ Mariners of the place at leaft, whether they have fhips or not; So as now we have neither fhips nor Mariners fufficient for our Trade, we upon the Matter exclude the Trading Part of the World from Trading with us, from whence thefe Confequences follow.

Confequences.

1. That the Growths and Manufactures of *England* to be exported in Forein Trade, are reduced to a few *Englifh* Merchants, who may take what they pleafe, and at what terms they pleafe; and leave the reft upon the poor Natives hands, without any other poffible means of Relief. So as our Native Commodities are not valuable as if Trade were free, but as a few Merchants pleafe to fet a price upon them.

2. As in our Native Commodities, fo in Forein, the Merchant and Natives of the place may impofe what rates they

they pleafe; and in the mean time, we exclude multitudes and concourfe of men and Traders, which would infinite-ly advance our Trade thereby; and now we complain for want of Trade, when as by this Law it feems impoffible to be otherwife.

3. As this Law makes a few Merchants Mafters of all the Trade of *England*: fo it makes Mariners the Merchants Mafters; for being but few, and the Merchant being reftrai-ned to them, if he gives not them what wages they pleafe, he muft not trade at all.

Annotations upon the Act of Navigation in general.

1. The Title of this Act is an Act for encouraging and encreafe of fhipping, yet it reftrains the Navigation of *Engl.* to *Englifh* built fhips, upon no lefs penalty than confifcati-on; whereas for above 120 years the want and decay of Timber hath been complained of in Parliament: and how then this can be a means to increafe fhipping, efpecially when we have fo few builders; I fhall be glad to be in-formed. But the confequences of Laws of like nature have been obferved and reflected upon. For by the 4 H. 7. 10. No *Gafcoyn* wine, or *Tholoufe* woad was to be imported into *England*, but in Ships *Englifh, Irifh, Welch*, or of the men of *Barwick* or *Callice*, and the Mr. and grea-ter part of the Mariners to be Subjects of the Realm of *England*, upon pain to forfeit the faid Wine and Woads; which was fuppofed to be made for the maintenance of the Navy of this Realm; and that the faid Wines and Woad might be had at more eafie prizes. The experience whereof has ever fince appeared to the contrary; for that the fa'd Wines and Woad were fold at fuch exceffive rates as had not been before feen within this Realm, and the Navy thereby never the better maintained; and therefore the Stat. of 4 H. 7. 10. was repzaled by the 5. and 6. Ed. 6 18. And liberty for all ftrangers in Amity with the King, as well as Subjects, to import the faid Wine and Woad.

By the 5 R. 2. 3. None of the Kings Subjects might carry forth or bring in any Merchandize but only in Ships of the

Laws of like nature found by experience mifchievous to this Nation.

Kings

Kings Allegiance; this was repealed by the 1 *Eliz* 13. because that by reason thereof there hath not only grown great
displeasure betwixt Forein Princes and the Kings of
this Realm, but also the Merchants have been sore grieved
and damaged.

The impossi-
bility of Exe-
cuting the Act
of Navigation.
Though the 5 of *R.* 2. 3. did not permit the Kings subjects to trade but in ships of the Kings Allegiance; yet by
the 6 *Rich.* 2. 8. where no *English* ships were to be had,
English men might trade in strangers ships and though by
the 4 *H.* 7. 10. *Gascoin* Wine, and *Tholouse* Woad, might
not be brought into the Realm but by the *English* Ships, and
English Merchants and Mariners; yet if they could not have
Fraught in an *English* or Den'zens Ships, they might fraught
a Strangers; whereas by the Act of Navigation; though
we have not built one Ship for the Trades of *Greenland*, *Norway*, nor *Muscovy*, since the Act of Navigation. Yet if we
buy any, or Fraught any Strangers Ship for any of the Trades,
it is forfeit with all her Goods, Guns, Lading, Tackle, and
Ammunition. So that though we may possibly have some
Trade to *Norway* for Timber, when our Prize Ships are spent,
upon such terms as the *Norwegians* please and not otherwise:
yet it will be impossible to have any Trade to *Muscovy* or
Gronland; for the *Muscovite* Trades not with us, and the
Whales have no Shipping at all.

*Other Mischiefs and Inconveniences which have ensued the Act
of Navigation.*

All the mis-
chiefs com-
plained of 17
Car. 11.
brought upon
us by this Law.
The 17 *Car.* 21 complains, that the Importation of Gun-
powder from Forein Parts, was against Law prohibited, and
the making thereof within this Realm ingrossed, whereby
the price of Gunpowder was excessively raised, many Powder Mills decayed, the Kingdom very much weakened and
indangered, the Merchants thereof much damnified, many
Mariners and others taken Prisoners, and brought into mi-
serable Captivity and Slavery: Many Ships taken by Turkish
and other Pirates, and many other inconveniences have from
thence ensued, and more are like to ensue, if they be not
                                                        timely

timely prevented ; and therefore this Law permits the Trade free to Strangers, as well as *English* to import Gunpowder : and though this Law stands yet in force, yet against it and all the reasons in it, the Act of Navigation makes it no less than confiscation of Ship, Goods, Guns, Tackle, and Ammunition for any *English* man to import any unless in an *English* built Ship, and Sailed by $\frac{3}{4}$ *English* at least , or for any Stranger, not Native of the making it, to import any, whether he hath Ships or not.

Prop. 7. Theorem 7.

The Trade of *England* is diminished by the Acts made 18. and 20. *Car.* 2: against the Importation of *Irish* Cattle,

Subject, Is the Trade of *England.*

Question, *Whether it be diminished by the Act against the Importation of* Irish *Cattel?*

I say it is.

Ax. 5. For every thing will be so much diminished, as is abated of it.

Pet, 21. But the Act against Importation of *Irish* Cattel, hath abated the Trade of *England ;* with *Ireland* for Hops and Beer, and in Returns of Mony by Bills of Exchange, Cloth, Stuffs of all sorts, Hats and Stockings of all sorts, Victualling Ships, *&c.*

Therefore the Act against Importation of *Irish* Cattel hath diminished the Trade of. *England.* Which was to be demonstrated.

Annotations upon this Proposition.

The reason of this Act, is by the Preamble expressed to be the lowness of the Rents of *England,* caused by the multitudes of *Irish* Cattel imported into *England.* It is true, the Evidence of Fact, is ever resolved by the testimony of Witness ; but this is ever done without reason, and therefore for strengthening the Authority of him who testifies, the Name of God is usually invoked , that what is affirmed, is

true ;

true; but in reasoning the Testimony of no man is more
than another, but as the Question in reason, is resolved by
antecedent Causes; nor herein is any man allowed to out-
sware another, who gives a better reason, by the 7. *Pet.*
multitudes and concourse of people advance Trade , and
scarcity of people diminish Trade : and therefore if all men
should affirm that a great Trade should be made where people
are scarce and thin, this should never prevail with me, since
it is against the nature of Trade; but on the contrary where
people are scarce and thin they are rude, Flat, Heathenish,
idle, and ever poor; and when they take great pains, which
is very rare, for want of Education it is to little purpose. By
the first Proposition, The multitudes of the *English* diverted
into our Plantations, hath diminished as well the Fishing
Trade as the Trade of our Native Growths and Manufactures;
which is more diminished by our re-peopling *Ireland*, since the
late War and Massacre there; and so much more diminished by
how many extraordinarily died of the late great Plague; and
by the 6 *Proposition*, the Growths and Manufactures of *England*
in Forein Trade are diminished by the Act of Navigation,
and multitudes and entercourse of Foreiners are excluded by
it, whereby the Trade of *England* is every way interrupted
and diminished : And since the Rents of Land are valuable,
as the Trade of the place is ; It is from hence that the Rent
of Land is so abated and fallen all over *England*, but much
more since the Act against Importation of *Irish* Cattel; so
as the end designed by the Law, which was the raising the
Rents of Land, is so far from being attained, that from these
Reasons the Trade of *England* being more diminished by this
Law, the quite contrary hath ensued.

One of the Reasons alledged by the Act intituled, *An Act
for the Encouraging of Trade*, made the 14 *Car.* 2. for the excluding Foreiners to Trade to our Plantations, is, to hold a
greater kindness and nearer Correspondency between the
English Nation and them, which reason of mutual kindness
I am sure will hold stronger between the *English* Nation and
Ireland; for if we lose them, or any of them, we lose no
more than the Subjects in them, who unless it be in reference

to Trade, are of no ufe to *England* ; whereas if by reafon of this Act, we lofe *Ireland*, or any part of it, the fafety of this Nation will be endangered thereby.

If the Importation of *Irifh* Cattel had abated the Rents of *England* one half, and thereby the Commodities of *England* had been reduced to half the price ; the Nation had not been poorer thereby, however the Nobility and Country Gentlemen who were in Debt, and the Poor Tenants who had Leafes of their Farms, would have been damnified and undone thereby : but in General, Navigation and the Trade of the Nation would have been advantaged by it.

The Reafons in the Act of Navigation are good for *England* againft Foreiners Trading into our Plantations ; and fo is the reftraining them from the Trade of *Ireland* ; for otherwife other Nations, efpecially the *Dutch*, would have reaped more benefit by them than we fhould have done : but without queftion our *Plantations* and *Ireland* too would have been much increafed and inriched by a Free Trade, more than by this reftraint ; and by like Reafon the Trade of *England* too would have been much more, and the Nation much more enriched than now, if no reftraint had been put upon the Trade by the Act of Navigation. For by the Act of Navigation the greater Trading part of the World are excluded the Trade of *Ireland* ; and by the Act againft Importation of *Irifh* Cattel, upon the matter the Trade between *England* and *Ireland* is interrupted and deftroyed : and here let us fee the Confequences hereof.

Confequences.

The Imaginary Reafon that the Importation of *Irifh* Cattel caufed the abatement of the Rents of *England* is truly caufed by the Act in the Southern and Eaftern parts of *England* : for the Northern People, *Welch*, and *Scots* taking advantage of this Law, have raifed the price of lean Cattel fo exceffively, that very fmall or no profit arifes to the Graziers, when they are Fatted. So as before the Act, we bought cheap and fold cheap, which was but reafonable ; whereas now we buy dearer and fell cheaper, which is intolerable.

2. Be-

2. Before the Act we could Victual Ships with good and fubftantial Food cheaper than the *Dutch*, and upon all occa-fions the *Dutch* and *French*, and other Nations when they were in our Harbours, did take a very confiderable quantity of our Provifion; whereas fince the Act the *Dutch* and *French* Victual much cheaper in *Ireland*, than we can do in *England*; and in *Holland* and *Zealand Irifh* Beef I am told by Traders thither is fold for a peny a pound; fo as having, as the cafe ftood, but one advantage above the *Dutch*, (befides the excellency and conveniencies of our Harbours) in Na-vigation; by this Law we have given the *Dutch* a greater ad-vantage over us than we had over them.

3. Before this Act, the Eaftern and Southern parts of *England* did in a very confiderable manner fupply *Flanders*, *France*, *Portugal*, and *Spain* with Butter, which now we have interrupted the intercourfe of Trade between *England* and *Ireland*, we have thereby put the *Irifh* upon neceffities of making Butter, which they do fo much cheaper than is pof-fible to be done in *England*, notwithftanding the abatement of our Rents, that they fupply *Flanders* and *France* much cheaper than the *Englifh* can; whereby our Trade for Butter and Cheefe is become much worfe than that of Grazing of Cattel: and now the *Irifh* have eftablifhed thefe Trades, much more advantageous to them than their Trade was to us with their lean Cattel: I underftand no remedy hereof, but they will increafe their advantages, and we muft yet more continue lofers.

4. Befides the abatement of our Native Growths and Ma-nufactures, caufed by the Act againft the Importation of *Irifh* Cattel, as *England* was the Storehoufe for all forts of Commodities coming from our Plantations, and other Fo-rein Goods, as all forts of Dying ftuffs, Hides, Fruit, Su-gars, Tobacco's, and of all forts of Silks as well wrought as unwrought, Ribbands, Gold, Silver, and Silk-Lace; fo the Trade with *Ireland* was driven by Commutation of the Pro-duct of the mony for their Lean Cattel; which being now interrupted, this Trade of *England* with *Ireland* for thefe be-comes proportionably leffened and diminifhed. Whereas

now

now they tranfport their Beef into *France, Holland, Zealand,* and *Flanders,* they make returns in the Growths and Manufactures of thofe Countries ; whereby the *Irifh* Trade is become as beneficial to them , as it was formerly to us.

5. His Majefties Cuftom for the Lean Cattel is quite extinguifhed.

6. The Shipping and Mariners imployed and built for this Trade, are by this Act neglected, and made ufelefs, about 100 Ships being before imployed in this Trade only.

7. That as before *Englifh* Shipping was generally imployed in the Trade with *Ireland,* fo the returns out of *Ireland* in Hides, Tallow, Wools, and Yarn into Forein parts was in *Englifh* Shipping ; whereas now we have not only loft the Profitable Returns of thefe Commodities, but Forein Ships are only imployed in thefe Trades.

Propofition 8. *Theorem* 8.

The Trade of *England,* and the Fifhing Trade are fo much hindred, by how many men, and fo much mony and ftock as are excluded by Corporations.

Subject, The Trade of *England,* and the Fifhing Trade.

Queftion, Whether they be fo much hindered, by how many men, and fo much mony and ftock as is excluded by Corporations?

I fay they are.

Ax. 6. For any bufinefs will be fo much hindered , by how much the means of improving it are excluded.

Pet. 13. But men are neceffary to improve Trade , and *Pet.* 5. mony is a convenient mean to improve Trade ; and *Pet.* 12. ftock is a convenient mean to improve Trade.

Therefore the Trade of *England,* and the Fifhing Trade are fo much hindered by how many men and fo much mony and ftock as are excluded by Corporations. Which was to be demonftrated.

Annotations.

So as the Trade of *England*, and the Fifhing Trade are diminifhed by our *American* Plantations, by the re-peopling *Ireland*, and the late great Plague, and our late Forein and inteftine Wars: It is hindered by the Act of Navigation in Forein Trade abroad, and the greater Trading part of the world are excluded from Trading with us at home; and the greater part of the Nation excluded from Trading at all, unlefs it be upon fuch terms as they cannot be any ways encouraged in it: whereas in the mean time Supernumeraries of Solicitors, Bankers, Scriveners, and Uferers, who inftead of Trading, divert all the means of improving Trade, and engrofs (I am confident) above fix times as much mony as is imployed in Trades beneficial to the Nation; and I believe are more than the free Trading part of the Nation.

For my part as I defire the good of the Nation in what I have faid, free from any paffion or affection to any party or perfon; fo do not I intend the prejudice, but good of every Corporation: for if men, mony, and ftock be the only means to enrich and ftrengthen any place, then every Corporation is fo much more capable of Riches and Strength, by how many more men, and fo much more mony and ftock is imployed in Trade. The *Dutch* (who of all the world are the moft confiderable, and richeft, and moft mighty by Trade) underftand this; and therefore *Amfterdam* (of all other places the moft famous for Trade) is now defigned to be enlarged ⅔ with free liberty for all the world to Plant and Trade with them. In or about the years 1636. and 37. about 140 Families out of the Counties of *Norfolk* and *Suffolk*, forfook us and went into *Holland*, where the *Dutch* did not only entertain them, but in *Leyden*, *Alkmere*, and other places, planted them Rent-free, and Excife-free for feven years.

Corollary.

By the fame reafon Forein Trade will be fo much hindered,

ed, by how much the means of Tranfporting mony in it are excluded.

Pet. 13. For mony is a convenient mean to improve Trade.

The *Dutch, Venetians*, and *Florentines*, who underftand this, and have no mony of their own, freely permit the Exportation of mony in Trade, and grow rich thereby, and the King of *Spain*, who hath all the Treafure of the *Weft-Indies*, upon the penalty of Death, &c. forbids the Exportation of it, grows poorer, and can keep none. Mr. *Mun* (a man of excellent knowledge and experience in Trade) in the 4th. Chapter, of *Englands Treafure by Forein Trade*, affirms, he knew a Prince in *Italy* (of famous memory) *Ferdinando* the Firft, great Duke of *Tufcany*, who being very rich, endeavoured thereby to enlarge his Trade by iffuing out to his Merchants great fummes of mony for very fmall profit: He himfelf had of the Duke 40000 Crowns *gratis* for a whole year, although the Duke knew it would be fent away in *fpecie* for the parts of *Turkey*, to be imployed in Wares for his Country. Afterwards Mr. *Mun* affirms he knew *Legorn* fo much increafed, that of a poor little Town it was become a fair and ftrong City, being one of the moft famous places for Trade in all Chriftendom. And yet it is worthy obfervation that the multitude of Ships and Wares, which come from *England*, the Low-Countries, and other places, have little or no means to make returns from thence but only ready mony. See more herein in the faid Chapter. Though Trade may be maintained by barter of Commodities, yet he who Trades in mony and barter, fhall have a vaft advantage.

Propofition 9. Theorem 9.

In the Trade of *England* with *France*, the *Englifh* Nation lofes fo much as the value of the *French* Commodities imported,

ported exceed the *English* exported , which Mr. *Fortry* affirms to be above 1600000 *l.* yearly:

Subject is, The *English* Nation.

Question, Whether it loses so much by the Trade with France, *as the value of the* French *Commodities Imported exceed the* English *Exported?*

I say it does.

Ax. 7. For where the consumption of things Imported, does exceed in value the things Exported , the loss will be as the excess is.

Pet. 2. But the *English* Nation consumes all the Commodities of *France* imported.

Pet. 3. And they exceed the Commodities of *England* Exported 1600000 *l.* a year, if Mr. *Fortry* hath truly computed it.

Therefore the *English* Nation loses so much as the excess is. Which was to be demonstrated.

Annotations upon this Proposition.

Nor is this all the loss the *English* Nation sustains by the Trade with *France* ; for Trading for *French* Wines in the perillous Months for Navigation of *September* , *October*, *November*, and *December*, we lose more Shipping and Sea-men in acquiring of them, than in all our other Trades besides ; and in our immoderate drinking of them , we more than ordinarily dispose our bodies to the Strangury , Fevers, Gout, and Stone, when they are pure : and to so many more Diseases as when they are so many ways sophisticated and adulterated by Vintners; so that instead of drinking Health to the King of *England*, we drink Sickness to our selves, and Wealth to the *French* King.

So that Reader thou mayest understand, what vast Revenues the *English*, and the *Dutch* much more than the *English*, yearly bring into *France* by their Trade with it. For though the *Dutch* Trade, (for Reasons hereafter specified) be not managed to the loss of the *Dutch*, as the *English* is; yet I am confident, and have it by good Authority , that if a true
esti-

eſtimate were made of it, it would appear to be above ſix-fold more beneficial to *France* than the *Engliſh* Trade is. Sir *Walter Rawleigh* takes notice that the *Dutch* Trade into all Ports and Creeks of *France*, we chiefly into 5 or 6, and in thoſe the *Dutch* have 4 times the Trade we have. So that if the *French* King can eſtabliſh a Spice Trade, wherein he is wonderouſly induſtruous, being King of a Flouriſhing Country, he will have but little occaſion to Export any Treaſure, nor need he fear but the *Engliſh* and *Dutch* will ſtill continue carriers of all the Wealth they get by *Spain*, and other places, into *France.*

Conſequences.

From hence it is that the *French* King becomes ſo rich above any other Prince or State in Chriſtendom; and being Prince of a noble and brave Kingdom, which abounds with moſt things conducing to the benefit of Humane Life, and very fruitful of men, as well as other things; and having few conſiderable Plantations to exhauſt his men; he becomes not leſs Potent and formidable to all Chriſtendom, than Rich and Glorious. Nor can I ever hope (the Pride and Luxury of the *Engliſh*, and the neceſſities of the *Dutch*, are ſuch) to ſee this vaſt increaſe of Wealth by the *Engliſh* and *Dutch* Trade with *France* to be abated; and what the further conſequences hereof will be in time, it is more than time to be conſidered both by the *Engliſh* and *Dutch*.

Corollary.

By the ſame Reaſon the *Engliſh* Nation loſes ſo much as the *Canary* Wines Imported exceed in value the *Engliſh* Commodities Exported into the *Canaries*; which if the value conſumed be 260000 *l.* yearly, and our Commodities do not amount to near 65000 *l.* yearly, we loſe above 195000 *l.* by this Trade.

Pet. 22. For we conſume all the *Canary* Wines Imported.

Pet. 23.

Pet. 23. And the *Canary* Wines imported, do exceed in value, the *Englifh* Commodicies Exported.

Annotations upon this Corollary.

So as having loft thofe gainful and beneficial Trades to *Mufcovy*, *Groenland*, and *Norway* too upon the matter, which is not longer lived if things muft ftand as now they do, than our Prizes taken in the late War laft; having loft our Fifhing Trade, more worth than all our Trades befides; and the *Turkey*, *Spanifh*, and *Guiny* Trades, and up the *Elb*, are now no longer ours : the *Dutch*, unlefs in the *Turkey* Trade, and up the *Elb*, are more Mafters than we, and fo in a fhort time are like to be in thefe too. We flonrifh in the *French* Trade, and are fo folely poffeffed of the *Canary* Trade, as we admit of no competitor:

Confequences.

From this wild and vaft expence by the *Englifh* in the *French* and *Canary* Trades, does follow a neglect and contempt of all our Native Cloth, Stuff, and other Manufactures, and our Liquors; the *French* Silks, Fine Linnen, and Lace are preferred in all our Debaucheries : he is efteemed a Clown, if the excefs be not in Sack and Claret, *&c.* And what now can the poor Country man expect in reward of all his labours, efpecially if he hath a Leafe, but to ruine himfelf and Family, by his labour and pains, for others who by their Prodigality and Luxury, undo themfelves and the Nation as well as the poor men?

Lemma.

So as Reader thou mayeft understand; (as *Mafter Mun* obferves) that the Kings Cuftoms, and particular men may grow rich by a Trade, whereby the Nation is impoverifhed : for Merchants, Vintners, Drawers,

Drawers, Exchange people, *&c.* grow Rich, and live higher than other men ; but the Nation droops, and in a very short time will be beggered by them . Nor must you, Reader, take your Meafures of our Trade, by the rife and fall of the Kings Cuftoms ; for unlefs Trade be freer here than in other places, and that the greatnefs of the Cuftoms arifes from the greatnefs of the Trade, not the greatnefs of the Impofitions, the higher the Cuftoms the worfe the Trade; for all muft be confumed in the place : and though the Cuftoms be now eight times more than in Queen *Elizabeths* Reign ; yet being upon Tobacco's, Sugars, Wine, and *French* Toys, the Nation is fo far from being enriched thereby, that it is fo much the poorer by how much men debauch themfelves by excefs in them.

Apology.

I do not defire to be underftood, as if I did intend any diminution to his Majefties Revenue by what is faid of the height of Cuftoms in this *Lemma* ; and therefore, though the influence , which height of Cuftoms has upon Trade, and the advantages, which the *Dutch* States reap by the lownefs of their Cuftoms be the fubject of another Propofition : Yet that I be not mif-apprehended, I fay, That if the Impofitions, which are now paid in Cuftoms were paid by way of Excife, as they are in the *United Netherlands*, thefe benefits, his Majefty as well as the Merchant would have. 1. His Majefties Revenue, as the cafe ftands, would be as much as now, unlefs in Exportation by Certificate, which is not much confiderable. 2. As the Trade and Traders by the lownefs of Cuftoms would increafe, fo would his Majejefties Revenue proportionably: whereas Trade diminifhing by the height of Cuftoms, fo muft his Majefties Revenue. 3. The Duties impofed upon Cuftoms, when they are high, excite men to ufe all means to fteal them , whereby they get fo much as they conceal ; whereas if the Cuftoms be low, men would not run like hazard to get little or nothing thereby. 4. The Merchant would be free to imploy his
mony

mony he pays in Cuftoms, in his Trade upon occafions, as they are offered. But if fo much as is impofed upon Exportation by Certificate, were impofed upon the Cuftoms, and the Cuftoms as they ftand were collected by Excife, the Kings Revenue would be the fame, and improvable as Trade would thereby improve; and the Merchant have the benefit of imploying all the mony he pays in Cuftoms in his Trade.

From the lownefs of Cuftoms and height of Excife it is, that though the *Englifh* Nation be capable of a ten-fold greater Trade than the *United-Netherlands*, yet the Revenue the *Dutch* States acquire hereby, is above three-fold more than the Kings Revenue by Excife and Cuftoms.

Epi-

Epilogue.

THus Reader thou mayeſt underſtand, that though *England* be the moſt excellent and convenient place for Trade of all others, yet our practice and ordering it, is contrary to the nature of it; which ever flouriſhes moſt in convenient places, where it is more free, and people more abound. The abundance of our people (beſides thoſe which the hand of God hath taken away) are diminiſhed in peopling our Plantations, and in re-peopling *Ireland* ſince the late War and Maſſacre there: So as thereby the ſtrength as well as Trade of the Nation is abated proportionally: and yet as matters ſtand, we have interrupted our Trade with *Ireland*: Nor can we for the future expect any great benefit from the Trade to our Plantations for Tobacco's and Sugars. For the *Dutch* by the late Treaty at *Breda* being poſſeſſed of *Surinam*, which yields better Sugars than our *Barbadoes*, and may do in a much more inexhauſtible manner, being upon the Continent, and as good Tobacco's as our *Virginia*; and being better Maſters of Trade than we are, and having no Laws of Naturalization, to reſtrain them from peopling it, and ſupplying themſelves at home; we for the future can expect little other comfort from our Plantations than to ſupply our ſelves with Sugars and Tobacco's, but muſt leave the *Dutch* to enrich themſelves with ſupplying the world thereby. Already the ‖*Dutch*, upon expectation of ſupplying themſelves with great quantities of Sugar and Tobacco's from *Surinam*, decline buying the Sugars of our Plantations; whereby they are become a Drug, and fallen from 42 *s.* a hundred, to 26. This puts the Sugar Bakers on new projects, *viz.* the boiling up of *Panellis* Sugar to ſupply and ſerve inſtead of looſe *Liſbon* Sugar, which was the principal Commodity returned in lieu of our Bays, Sayes, Searges, and Perpetuanoes, there

vended

vended in great quantities, and for want of returns by exchange not to be there obtained, the value principally returned in *Lisbon* Sugar; so as our Native Commodities in
the *Lisbon* Trade too must in a short time not fall only, but
want vent.

As *Ireland* and our Plantations have exhausted our men
whereby our Trade and strength is abated and diminished, so the Law against Naturalization debars any future
supply of other men from Planting with us; and the Law of
Navigation excludes much the greater Trading part of the
world from Trading with us from abroad, and our Corporations restrain our Trade to as few at home: so as Trade,
which ever flourishes in multitude and freedom, is by us, by all
imaginable ways circumscribed, taxed, and reduced to a few.

While we are contriving newer and more severe Laws
against the Exportation of Wool, and neglect the careful
inspection and management of our Woollen Manufactures,
whereby they have lost their Reputation abroad; we put the
world upon necessities of supplying themselves elsewhere,
and especially from *Ireland*: whereby the *Dutch* not only
partake with us in our *Turkey* Trade, and up the *Elb*; but the
Dutch and *French* in our own Markets in *England* have a free
and open Trade in Woollen Cloths and Stuffs; and in the
mean while our Wool becomes a Drug, and of no price or
esteem at home: whereby, notwithstanding the severity of
all our Laws against the Exportation thereof, great quantities are exported; and so will be until we establish such a
Trade in our Woollen Manufactures, that men shall be better encouraged to work them here than elsewhere; for all
men will rather venture their lives than lose their means of
living.

We neglect to give any encouragement in assisting Ingenuous and Industrious men in any undertaking for the Publick good. I give one instance in the County of *Suffolk*, and
here in *Clerkenwel*: The *English* during the late *Dutch* and
French War, did betake themselves to Weaving Poldavies, or
Buck, which they did make into double Buck, being two
threds spun together, and made of our *English* Hemp,
(which

(which *Ipfwich* and *Woodbridge* men affirm to be better than any Eaft Country Hemp for this ufe) which made better Sails than any other, and did manage a confiderable Trade thereby, to the great benefit of *Suffolk*: but now the *Dutch* and *French* Buck is fold fomewhat cheaper (the *Englifh* not being as yet fo much Mafters of the Trade as the *Dutch* and *French*.) This Trade begins to decline again, and to be neglected for want of fome fmall Encouragement, which might be done by fome fmall Impofition, for fome time upon the *French* and *Dutch* Buck, until we fhould be enabled to work it as cheap, as it is in *France* and *Holland*.

As we give no encouragement to our induftrious Natives, fo we utterly difcourage all induftrious Foreiners from improving and increafing Trade. I need not here repeat the difcouragement put upon the Silk-throwers by the Corporation and Company of *London*, wherein near 20000 people are imployed; though the firft introduction of Silk-throwing was by a Foreiner, the worthy Father of Sir *Thomas Chamberlain*, now a worthy Citizen of *London*, becaufe the Wifdom of Parliament hath provided fecurity for the Silk-throwers.

But though the Weaving Silk be as much or more advantageous to the Nation, yet certain ingenuous and induftrious *French* Artificers, who endeavoured to exercife their Trades laft Summer in the Suburbs of *London*, were Indicted at *Hicks-Hall*, by certain of the Yeomanry of the Company of Weavers, Commiffionated by the Bailiff, Warden, and Affiftants of the faid Company, and committed to the *New-Prifon* in *Clerkenwel*; though the difference between the faid Company and the Proteftant Strangers ufing manual Occupation, was upon the Addrefs of the *French* and *Dutch* Churches, depending before his Majefty and Council. Nor could any relief herein be had, though his Majefty in Council the 29. of *October* laft referred the bufinefs to the Lords of the Committee of Trade, until his Majefty in Council the 10th. of *November* laft, was pleafed to difcharge them.

I need not here recite the benefits the Nation at this day reaps by the permitting the *Walloons* to eftablifh their Trades

at

at *Canterbury*, *Norwich*, *Colchester*, and other places : the Nation (at leaft the Southern and Eaftern parts) know they are the beft Trades we have now left : Yet I cannot but take notice that within the memory of man, the returns of *Maidftone* Market did not amount to weekly above 30 *l.* whereas fince, admitting about 60 Families of Foreiners in the thred Trade, the returns are weekly now above 1000 *l.* to the incredible benefit of the Lands, as well as all forts of people adjoyning.

How pernicious this practice of excluding Foreiners muft needs be to the Nation, as it now ftands, if it be continued, is underftood by his Majefty. And the *French* King fo well underftands how much it will conduce to the advantage of *France* to encourage the freedom of Trade, by entertaining all forts of Forein Artificers, that in contradiction to all the Ecclefiaftical Powers oppofing it, he hath granted free liberty to all forts of Forein Artificers and Merchants to exercife their Confciences in all Ports and places in his Dominion, and to have Churches allowed them with equal or more Priviledges than his natural Subjects. Sure now it will be no ways prudent in us fo to difcourage any herein, as to be entertained by the *French* King, as well as *Dutch*.

So that all the good and beneficial ends defigned by Trade , *viz* of imploying all forts of Impotent People, Women, and Children ; of Strengthning, and enriching our felves by Trade are quite inverted by us. For the Fifhing Trade, and the Trades of Making Dying and Drefling our Cloaths and Stuffs, wherein all forts of poor people might have been imployed, is loft and neglected by us , whilft we intend the *Newcaftle* Trade, the *French, Canary, Turkey, Eaft-India* Trade, and to our Plantations, wherein only lufty men are imployed, and the Impotent People, Women, and Children are expofed to beggery, and the publick charge. Secondly, *Ireland* and our Plantations Rob us of all the growing Youth and Induftry of the Nation, whereby it becomes week and feeble, and the Strength, as well as Trade , becomes decayed and diminifhed, I, and the Law againft Naturalization Bars us of any future fupply: And thirdly, Our

Affluence,

Affluence, Luxury, and irregular management of Trade, renders us poorer, and in a worfe condition, than if we had no Trade at all.

So as here, Reader, thou mayeft underftand the reafon of the decay and falls of the Rents of Lands in *England*; for by the 11 *Petition,* the Rents of Lands are valuable as the Trade of the place is: the Trade of *England* therefore being diminifhed, the Rents of the Lands in *England* are confequently fallen and diminifhed in proportion to it.

THE

REASONS

OF THE

INCREASE

OF THE

Dutch-Trade.

PART II.

Wherein is Demonſtrated from what cauſes the Dutch *govern and manage Trade better than the* Engliſh, *whereby they have ſo far improved their Trade above the* Engliſh.

Petitions.

1. MEN labour more induſtriouſly in Trade , and upon eaſier terms in the *United Netherlands* than in *England.*

2. The *Dutch* have down the *Rhine*, *Maez*, and *Scheld*, out of *Germany*, *France*, *Lorrain*, *Flanders*, and other *Spaniſh* Provinces, greater quantities of Timber, more choice, and upon leſs terms than can be had in *England*, but more ſince the Timber

of

of *England* is so much diminished by the Act of *Navigation*, and much more when the City of *London* is rebuilt.

3. The *Dutch* have Pitch, Tar, Hemp for Cordage, Tackle, and Iron, in greater quantities, and for less terms than the *English* can, out of *Norway*, *Denmark*, and other Kingdoms within the *Sound*.

4. Pitch, Tar, Cordage, Tackle, and Iron are necessary means in fitting up Ships for Navigation.

5. The *Dutch* build Ships for Navigation more conveniently than the *English*.

6. The *Dutch* acquire more Forein Commodities in Trade out of *Germany* cheaper and with more convenience, than the *English* do out of *Scotland*.

7. The whole world is Water and Land.

8. The *Dutch* pay less Customs for Forein Commodities at home than the *English*.

9. The *Dutch* pay less Customs for Forein Commodities in Forein Trade, than the *English* do.

10. The *Dutch* pay less interest for mony, than the *English*.

11. The *Dutch* States are more conversant in Trade than the Council of *State* in *England*, or any other.

12. The *Dutch* generally breed their youth of both Sexes in the Studies of Geometry and Numbers, especially more than the *English* do.

13. The Study of Geometry and Numbers, is the best Education for understanding Trade.

14. The *Dutch* States have equal or more means in Trade, than the Council of State in *England*, or any other.

15. A *Dutch* Statesman is more interessed in Trade than a Counsellor of State in *England*, or any else.

16. *Dutch* Merchants and their Wives are generally more conversant in Trade than the *English*.

17. *Dutch* Merchants have fewer impediments in Trade than *English*, and have their Controversies in Trade sooner determined, and with less charge and trouble.

18. The *Dutch* pay less Customs for their Domestick Manufactures in Forein Trade, than the *English* do.

Axioms

Axioms or Common Notions.

8. Where men labour more induſtriouſly upon leſs terms upon any thing, this thing is cheaper managed.

9. Any buſineſs which is more freely managed may be greatlier managed than if it were more reſtrained.

10. More buſineſs is done by more means, and cheap, if the means be had upon eaſier terms.

11. More buſineſs may be done by more means, and cheap, and more conveniently, if the means be more convenient and cheaper.

12. Who buyes cheaper than another, and more conveniently, may ſell cheaper, and with much more gain, if the charge be otherways leſs.

13. All things are either Forein or Domeſtick.

14. They who are more converſant in any buſineſs, and better Educated in it, may underſtand it better than another.

15. They who may underſtand any buſineſs better than another, may govern it better than that other.

16. Where men are more intereſſed in any buſineſs, they are leſs ſubject to be corrupted to the prejudice of it.

17. They who have fewer impediments in any buſineſs, and leſs charge and trouble in it, may improve it better than another who hath more.

18. The whole is equal to all parts.

TREA-

TREATISE II.

Propofition I. *Problem* I.

HOW the *Dutch* manage a greater Trade at home than the *Englifh*.

Subjects, Are the *Dutch* and *Englifh*.

Queftion, How the Dutch *manage a greater Trade at home?*

Conftruction. By the 1 *Pet.* 1. the *Dutch* freely enteitain men of all Nations in Trade, and give them equal priviledges with the natural born *Dutch* : By the 9 *Pet.* 1. The *Englifh* by the Bar of Naturalization and freedom of Strangers reftrain the Trade of *England* to the *Englifh* only. I fay the *Dutch* may manage a greater Trade at home,

Ax. 9. For any bufinefs which is more freely managed, may be, and is greatlier managed than if it were more reftrained.

Conft. But Trade is more freely managed by the *Dutch* at home than by the *Englifh*.

Therefore the *Dutch* manage a greater Trade at home. *which was to be done.*

Annotations.

From hence it is that the *Dutch* States without the danger of War, or putting themfelves into the power of fickle and unconftant Fortune, and by deftruction and devaftation of other Countries, killing and making men miferable by poverty and flavery, from no principles from within themfelves, but by acquiring men and means from other places, have attained the means (though all the *United Neatherlands* do not in bignefs exceed the County of *York* nor have half the conveniencies of that Country, except in numbers of people) to manage a greater Trade at home than any other Country

try of the world: It is true, the times since they became
States have concurred much to their advantage herein; for
entertaining all sorts of persons, who, upon the account of
either Religion or Faction, forsook their Countries, they
have been much more enabled to do this. But the Province
of *Holland* above all other, for no sort of people was de-
nyed admission there; whereby *Holland*, as it is of more
strength than all the other Provinces, so it contributes $\frac{4}{16}$
to all Publick Taxes.

Whereas this Nation does not only lye under the restraint
of the Bar of Naturalization, and *Ireland* and our Plantations are always open to exhaust us of our men: but besides
the multitudes of *English* which are dispersed in other places
of the *Netherlands*, *Rotterdam*, *Middleborough*, and *Flushing*,
are about $\frac{1}{4}$ *English*, and of *English* Extraction. About the
Years 1636. and 37. about 140 Families out of *Norfolk* and
Suffolk forsook us, and Planted themselves in *Leyden*, *Alkmen*,
and other places of the *United Netherlands*, and there established the Woollen Manufactures of those places, which at
this day is as much advantageous to the *Dutch*, and prejudicial to us, as Queen *Eliz.* (after the example of K. *Edward* 3.)
entertaining the *Walloons*, persecuted by the Duke of *Alva*,
and planting them in *Colchester*, *Norwich*, *Canterbury*, &c. was
advantageous to us, and prejudicial to the King of *Spain*:
And sure it is worthy the consideration of the Parliament
how this may be prevented for the future.

One *Thomas Tilham* born at *Martley* in the County of *Wor-
cester*, and formerly a Chirurgeon in *Warwick* treated with
the *Elector Palatine* of *Rhine*, about 6 years since to bring in a
Colony to Inhabit, and establish Woollen Manufactures in
the *Palatinate*; which the Prince allowing, the said *Tilham*
hath brought in a Colony of, its believ'd, between 2000 and
3000 men, who now manage a Trade upon Woollen Manufactures; and for *Tilhams* Reward herein, the Prince hath
made him Commander of them. Many of these people came
to *Tilham* out of *Essex* and *Suffolk*: One *Skip* of *Herefordshire*
is gone to him with some people; so are several others out of
those parts.

So

So that, though all Princes as well as States almost understood the wealth and strength which attends a Domestick Trade, as well as the *Dutch*; Yet we only of almost all the world are so careless herein, that we neither care for encreasing our Domestick Trade, nor to restrain our Artificers from betraying the mystery of ours: though the free admission of People of all Nations was the first Principle of the Greatness of the *Dutch* Domestick Trade, and the restreining our Domestick Trade to the *English* only, is the first Principle of the Decay of ours.

Prop. 2. Theorem 1.

The *Dutch* manage Trade cheaper in the United Netherlands than the *English* do in *Engl.*

Subjects, are the *Dutch* and *English* Nation.

Question, *Whether the* Dutch *manage Trade cheaper?*

I say the *Dutch* manage Trade cheaper.

Ax. 8. For where men labour more industriously and upon easier terms upon any thing, this thing is cheap managed.

Pet. 1. Lib. 2.

Pet. 1. *lib.* 2.
     But Men in the United Netherlands labour in Trade more industriously and upon easier Terms, than in *Engl.*

Therefore the *Dutch* manage Trade cheaper in the United Netherlands, than the *English* doe in *England.* Which was to be done.

Annot.

As the Law against Naturalization is the reason, why the *Dutch* in the United Netherlands, manage a greater trade, than the *English* do in *England*, so is it the reason, that Trade is cheaper managed there than in *England*. For if the Trade of *England* being managed by reason of this Law by *English* men only, who by reason of our Plantations, the Repeopling *Ireland*, the late great Plague, and our late Wars are thin and very few, if you will have any work in Trade done, you must

do it as the imployed *English* pleafe ; or you muſt have no
work done : whereas if the Trade of *England* were as freely
managed as in the United Netherlands, the *English* man then
muſt work and be as induſtrious as other men, or he muſt
not work at all : This freedome of managing Trade in the
United Netherlands, as it increaſes the hands there, ſo it
makes men more induſtrious in Trade ; for the multitudes
of people concurring in Trade an emulation of excelling one
another is excited , whereby every man endeavours to excel
the other in ſome way or other ; whereas in *England,* Trade
being circumſcribed by the few *English* in it ; they not only
work dearer, but are careleſs in working. Nor will I ever
believe that Induſtry is reſtreined to *English,* excluſive to o-
ther Nations. I cannot paſs over how much the Trade of
England is at this day bettered by Queen *Eliz.* prudent
Entertaining the *Dutch* and *Fleming* , againſt the Law of Naturalization ; who not being able to indure the inſupportable Tyranny of the Duke of *Alva ,* ſought refuge in this
Nation ; where in *Colcheſter,* *Norwich,* and *Canterbury,* they
were planted, and there they brought in thoſe Trades, where
at this day are the beſt we have left in *England.*

Prop. 3. Problem 12.

How the *Dutch* may and do build more Ships for Navigation, and cheaper than the *English.*

Subjects, are the *Dutch* and the *English.*

Queſtion, *How the* Dutch *may and doe build more Ships for
Navigation and cheaper than the* English ?

Conſtruction, The *Dutch* have down the Rhine, Maez, and
Sceld out of *Germany, France, Lorain, Flanders* and other
Spaniſh Provinces greater quantities of Timber, more choiſe
and upon leſs terms than can be had in *Engl* : but much more
ſince it is ſo much diminiſhed by the Act of Navigation, *Prop.3.lib. 1.*
and muſt be yet much more in rebuilding the City of *London.*
I ſay the *Dutch* may build more Ships, *&c.*

Ax. 10. For more buſineſs is done by more means, and
cheaper if the means may be had upon eaſier terms.

But

14. *Pet. lib.* 1.
Construction.

But Timber is a neceſſary mean in building Ships, and the *Dutch* have more Timber, more choiſe, and upon eaſier terms than the *Engliſh*.

Therefore the *Dutch* may and doe build more ſhips for Navigation, and cheaper then the *Engliſh*. Which was to be done.

Annotations.

It was proved before a Committee of the Houſe of Commons laſt Seſſion of Parliament, that the *Dutch* build ſhips of equal dimenſions for one half the *Engliſh* can; It is true that the goodneſs of our Timber heretofore when we had ſufficient, and choiſe, did in a great meaſure compenſate the charge in building Ships; in regard that Ships built of *Engliſh* timber were much more Durable and ſtrong: but now all our beſt Timber, is waſted and deſtroyed, and muſt be more in rebuilding the City of *London*, our Timber not coming to perfection in leſs then 150 years growth, if care were taken for the Preſervation and increaſe thereof, which I never hope to ſee; I doe not underſtand for the future how we ſhall poſſibly build ſo good Ships as either *Dutch*, *Dane*, or *French*, for three times the price: And ſo Reader I leave to thee to conſider the fatall conſequences like to enſue, upon this poor Nation in this thing only.

Prop. 4. Probl. 3.

How the *Dutch* may and do fit up more Ships for Navigation, and cheaper than the *Engliſh*.

Subjects, are the *Dutch* and *Engliſh*.

Queſtion, *How the* Dutch *fit up more Ships for Navigation and cheaper.*

Construction.
3 *Pet. lib.* 2.

The *Dutch* have Pitch, Tar, Hemp for Cordage, and Tackle, and Iron in greater quantities, and for leſs terms than the *Engliſh* can out of *Norway*, *Denmark*, and other Kingdoms within the Sound. I ſay the *Dutch* may fit up more Ships for Navigation, cheaper than the *Engliſh*.

A.x. 10.

Ax. 10. For more bufinefs may be done by more means
and cheaper, if the means may be had upon eafier terms.

But Pitch, Tar, Cordage, Tackle, and Iron, are neceffary
means in fitting up Ships for Navigation.

And the *Dutch* have more or greater Quantities of Pitch,
Tar, Cordage, Tackle, and Iron than the *Englifh*, and upon
eafier Terms,

Therefore the *Dutch* fit and doe up more Ships for Navigation, and cheaper than the *Englifh*. Which was to be
done.

Annotations.

Here muft I take notice that fince the Rumps inftitution
of the Act of Navigation the condition of fitting up fhips
for Navigation in *England* is as bad as the building of Ships,
and that againft the Act of the 1 *Eliz.* 13. which ftands
yet in force. For by the 1 *Eliz.* 13. It is free for all men
to import Pitch and Tar in any Veffels; whereas by the
Act of Navigation; if any *Englifh* man imports any Pitch,
or Tar unlefs in an *Englifh* built Ship, and failed by ¼ *Englifh* at leaft, now we have neither men nor Ships to do it,
the Ship is forfeit, Goods, Guns, Ammunition, and Tackle :
and fo it is in a ftrangers Ship who is not a Native of the
place, whereby he may impofe what terms he pleafe, or
otherwife we muft not have either Pitch or Tar at all : And
our Condition for Cordage and Tackle is much worfe, for
though we may have Pitch and Tar, upon fuch Terms as
the *Dane* and *Swede* pleafe : yet it will be impoffible in a
fhort time to have any Cordage or Tackle at all. For it
muft be imported by either *Englifh* men in *Englifh* Ships,
when we have neither men nor Ships to do it; or by the
Natives of the place, when the Inhabitants of *Riga, Revell,*
Narve and other places of *Leifland*, from whence all the
beft hemp (if not all) for Cordage and Tackle comes, trade
not with us at all.

Prop. 3.

Prop. 5. Problem 4.

How the *Dutch* may and do acquire more Forein Commodities by Navigation, cheaper and more conveniently than the *English*.

Subjects, are the *Dutch* and *English*.

Quest. *How the* Dutch, *ut supr.*

Construction. By the 3.*Prop.* 2. the *Dutch* may and doe build more ships and cheaper than the *English*, and by the 4 *Prop.* l. 2. they may fit up more ships and cheap, and by the 5 *Pet.* 2. they build Ships more conveniently: I lay the *Dutch* &c.

Ax. 11. For more business may be done by more means and cheaper, and more conveniently, if the means be more convenient and cheaper.

Conſt. But the *Dutch* may, and do build and fit up more ships, more conveniently and cheaper than the *English*.

15 Pet. 1. And Ships are neceſſary means in *Navigation*.

Therefore the *Dutch* may and doe acquire more Forein Commodities by Navigation cheaper and more conveniently than the *English*. Which was to be done.

Annotations.

So that as the *Dutch* build and fit out Ships cheaper than the *English*, ſo they build them more conveniently for Trade. For every Trade they build Ships, whereas in *England* unleſs it be in the Iſland Trade (wherein I do affirm are not one fourth part of the ſhipping in *England*, as was when the Act of Navigation had its firſt birth) all Ships ſerve for all Trades, the *Dutch* herein ſo far excell the *English* and all other Nations; that truly upon this account, they can, notwithſtanding the Impoſitions of the King of *Denmark* in the Trade of *Norway* for *Timber*, ſupply any part of the world cheaper than the King of *Denmarks* own Subjects, notwithſtanding the Aboundance of Timber and Pitch

and

and Tar, which so much abounds in *Norway*. This appeared in the time of *Oliver*, who permitting the *English* to Trade for Timber, Pitch, and Tar in Dutch bottoms, forced the *Norwegians* to sell the Ships they had built to Trade with the *English* for want of Employment; so in the years 1667, and 1668. the Kings permitting the *English* to trade in *Dutch* bottoms for Timber to *Norway*, and the *Dutch* to import it; reduced all the excessive Impositions which the King of *Denmark* had imposed upon the *English* before in that Trade, or otherwise he had undone his own Subjects.

And as in this Trade, so in all others, they so excell in the convenient building of Shipping; that Sir *Walter Rawleigh* in his observation on Trade, which he dedicated to King *James* near 60 years since, affirms, if an *English* Ship of 200 Tuns, and a *Holland* Ship of like burden be at *Danske* or any other place beyond the Seas, they serve the Merchant cheaper by a 100 *l.* by reason the *Hollands* Ship is sayl'd by 9 or 10 Mariners, and ours with near 30. Notwithstanding we yet continue our old way of building Ships, and so must so long as the Law against Naturilization stands in force; for the *English* know no other; and if the *English* Merchant will not build as the *English* Carpenter pleases, and his way, he must not Trade at all; for if he buyes and Trades in any Forein Ship, she is forfeit, Goods, Guns, Ammunition and Tackle by the Act of Navigation. So as the *Dutch* build Ships for half the price the *English* do, and Navigate for half the price. From whence it follows,

Consequences.

That though the *Dutch* much more than double about in Mariners above the *English*, yet navigating with much less than half the hands, they may drive above 4 times the Trade by Navigation: than the *English* doe; and building and fitting up their Ships for half the terms do navigate for half the price? from whence it is that though the Herrings (except red Herrings which cannot be cured by them) and
other

other Fish, be taken upon our Coast, the exportation of
them as free, as in the United Netherlands, yet cannot we
supply any part of the World so cheap as they; whereby
they have only left us the Trade of red Herrings, and to
supply our selves by excluding them, from trading with us,
with white Herring.

Probl. 6. Theorem 12.

The *Dutch* may and do acquire more Forein Commodities in Trade cheaper and with more convenience than the
English, in all the world.

Subject, The *Dutch*.

Question, *Whether they may acquire?* &c.

I say they may.

Ax. 18 For the whole is equal to all the parts.

Pet. 7. 2. But the whole world is Land and Water.

Prop. 5. 2. The *Dutch* acquire more Forein Commodities by water cheaper, and with more convenience.

Pet. 6. 2. And so do by Land.

Therefore the *Dutch* may and do acquire more Forein
Commodities in Trade cheaper and with more convenience
than the *English*. Which was to be demonstrated.

Prop. 7. Prob. 4.

How the *Dutch* may and do sell more Forein Commodities at home and in Forein Trade, cheaper, more conveniently, and with much more Gain than the *English*.

Subjects, Are the *Dutch* and *English*.

Quest. *How the* Dutch? *&c.*

Construction, By the 6. Prop. *lib.* 2. they acquire more
Forein Commodities in Trade, cheaper, and with more convenience; And *Pet.* 1. *lib.* 2. the *Dutch* pay less Customs
for Forein Commodities at home and in Forein Trade, and
10. *Pet.* 2. they pay less interest for mony.

I say the *Dutch* sell, &c.

Ax. 12.

Ax. 12. Who buyes cheaper than another and more conveniently, may fell cheaper, and with much more Gain, if the charge be otherwaies lefs.

Conftruction, But the *Dutch* buy more Forein Commodities cheaper, and more conveniently; and their charge is otherwife lefs in paying lefs cuftoms and lefs intereft for mony.

Therefore the *Dutch* may and do fell more Forein Commodities cheaper, more conveniently, and with much more Gain then the *Englifh.*Which was to be done.

Annotations.

Pay lefs Cuftomes, By reafon whereof principally the *Dutch* doe not only thrive by the Trade with *France,* but upon the matter their whole Trade is founded in it: For without the Salt of *France* the *Dutch* could not Fifh: and by the Fifhing Trade, the Wine, Salt, and Brandies of *France,* they drive their Trades into *Germany,* the Northern, and North-eaft Countries;from whence they draw thofe Commodities, whereby they are enabled to drive their Trades to *Spain,* into the Streights; and to the Eaft and Weft-Indies; whereas by the benefit of our Mony and Commodities we are only enabled to lofe about 1600000 *l.* a year, if Mr. *Fortry* hath truly compated it.

Nor is this all the Benefit the *Dutch* receive by the fmalnefs of their Cuftoms, which Sir *Walter Rawleigh* affirms not to be the 19 part fo much as the *Englifh,* (though in truth they are much lefs) yet by this means they draw all Nations to Traffick with them; and though the Duties they receive be but fmall; yet the multitudes of all forts of Commodities brought in by themfelves and others, and carried out by themfelves and others, is fo great that,they receive more Cuftoms and duties to their State in one year by the Greatnefs of their Commerce than *England* does in two by the greatnefs of their cuftoms.

And as this Monarchy by reafon hereof hath loft the Trade to a Common-wealth, fo by reafon hereof a Commonmonwealth in *Italy* hath lost their Trade to a Monarchy. For the State of *Genoa* imposing Customs upon 16 *per cent.* upon all Commodities imported, the Duke of *Florence* taking the advantage thereof by making *Legorn* a Free Port; whereby it is become one of the most famous and flourishing Towns in *Europe :* And the *Genoans* are forced to turn Usurers, upon what they had got before. And this year the King of *France* in probability hath laid a foundation to undo *Legorn* by making *Marselles* a free Port.

The King of *Sweeden*, within the memory of man, made *Gottenburg* a Free Port for 7 years, which at this day hath established such a Trade there, that of a poor and unregarded Village, it is become the most flourishing Town of Trade in the North, or North-East. Here Reader let me desire thee to partake some part of my Grief, in beholding such unsafe and barred Ports as *Gottenburg*, and all those of the *United Netherlands* to be by means of their freedom so Rich and Flourishing; whereas our most excellent, noble, and safe Harbours, but especially *Falmouth* (which *Cambden* prefers before *Brundusium*, or any other) and for its excellency and convenience, deserves to be the Store house of Christendom, yet hath scarce a Cock-boat belonging to it) are all neglected and passed by, by reason of the height of our Customs, the Laws of Naturalization and Navigation.

Pay less Interest for mony. By reason whereof the *Dutch* may preserve stores of all sorts of Commodities, and at any time sell them cheaper than the *English*, who pay more Interest for mony. Sir *Walter Rawleigh* affirms that *Amsterdam* is never without 700000 Quarters of Corn, besides the Plenty they daily vent: And that a Dearth of Corn in *England*, *France*, *Spain*, *Italy*, *Portugal*, or other places enriches *Holland* 7 years after : whereas we are only permitted to sell it, when cheap, to the no benefit of *England*, and to buy it when dear, to the impoverishing of us. Besides, it is impossible, when two or more Ships are imployed in any voyage, the one paying after the rate of 4 *per cent.* the other 6, if otherwise their charge be equal, that upon equal terms they can sell their Commodities, upon equal profit.

So that though the height of Cuſtoms and Intereſt of money, do both prejudice Trade, where it relates to any other place where either are leſs or lower; yet the height of Intereſt is more inſupportable, in that it every day increaſes; whether it be in preſerving Stores, or in reference to the length of Voyages in Forein Trade. And whereas the publick Revenue is augmented by the height of Cuſtoms, yet to the prejudice of Trade; ſo Trade is more prejudiced by the height of Intereſt, without any advantage to the publick Revenue. Nor does the miſchief of height of Intereſt mony end here, but it hath a like bad influence upon building, and fitting out Ships, where no Cuſtom is paid: So as a *Dutch* Ship of equal Dimenſions, may be built and fitted out to Sea for half the terms an *Engliſh* Ship can: and this Ship thus built and fitted up for half the terms, is ſailed with half the hands; ſo as this charge being both ways double to the *Engliſh,* and the *Engliſh* paying ⅟₇ Intereſt more, the *Engliſh* Merchant labours from hence, in a three-fold charge more than the *Dutch* Merchant does, and this not to be at one time diſcharged as Cuſtoms are, but ever to be impoſed upon the Ship ſo long as ſhe laſts: from whence it will neceſſarily follow, that if our Cuſtoms were lower than the *Dutch*, yet if the Intereſt of mony be in proportion higher, the *Dutch* may and will hereby only maintain the Trade of the world excluſive to the *Engliſh.*

Corollary.

By the ſame reaſon the *Dutch* may ſell more Domeſtick Manufactures at home, and in Forein Trade cheaper, and more conveniently than the *Engliſh*, and with much more gain.

For by the 2 *Prop. lib.* 2. Trade is cheaper managed in the *United Netherlands* than in *England*: and *Prop.* 1. *lib.* 2. It is more managed there than in *England:* And **18** *Pet.* 2. The *Dutch* pay leſs Cuſtoms for their Domeſtick Commodities in Forein Trade.

Prop. 8.

Prop. 8. *Theorem* 3.

The *Dutch* may sell more Commodities in Trade, than the *English*, cheaper, more conveniently . and with much more gain.

Subjects, Are the *Dutch* and *English*.

Question, *Whether the* Dutch *may and do sell,* ut supra ?

I say they may.

Ax. 13. For all things are either Forein or Domestick.

Proposition 7.2. But the *Dutch* may sell more Forein Commodities at home and abroad, cheaper, more conveniently, and with much more gain than the *English*.

Corollary.

And may sell more Domestick Manufactures at home, and in Forein Trade, cheaper, more conveniently, and with much more gain.

Therefore the *Dutch* may and do sell more Commodities in Trade, cheaper, more conveniently, and with much more gain than the *English*. Which was to be demonstrated.

Annotations.

They do it, and have done it, and are thereby become the greatest Prodigy that ever the world brought forth. For let any consider them in their first principles, being inconsiderable either for Number or Quality from their first rise, to be opposed by the most powerful Monarch in Christendom for near 80 years together! and from no principles of Trade from within themselves, nor having scarce a piece of Ground to build one house upon, nor one stick of Timber, or scarce one handful of Hemp, Pitch, Tar, or Iron, to build or fit out a Ship; and notwithstanding their constant Wars with *Spain*, to ingage and undertake so many Wars against the *Swede, Dane, Portugal,* and in the *East* and *West-Indies ?* To build so many fair and stately Cities beyond any other part of the World, and all
this

this in lefs than 100 years ; and at this day to manage a greater and more gainful Trade than all the world : whereby their
Wealth is ineftimable, and all this in contradiction to feem-
ing impoffibilities. Nor is their ftrength and power at Sea
lefs terrible, than their wealth ineftimable ; and at this day
all the Affairs almoft of Chriftendom are tranfacted at the
Hague : Queen *Eliz.* a Princefs of moft excellent Prudence and forefight, though fhe were carelefs in hindering
them in the progrefs of their Trade , yet was very vigilant
in reftraining their ftrength by Sea : nor would fhe permit
them to build many Men of War, and thofe not confiderable ; whereby without any controul fhe kept them in per-
fect fubjection at Sea. After King *James* loved peace, and his
Book fo well , that he did not reftrain their rifing power by
Sea. K. *Charles* (of Sacred memory) forefaw the danger of it,
and would have reftrained it , but it pleafed God he reigned
in fuch perverfe times , that he either was not, or, which was
worfe , could not be underftood by his Subjects : fo as now
their power at Sea is fwelled to fuch a prodigious greatnefs,
as it is a queftion whether it can be controuled by all the
power in the world ; and what the confequences hereof will
be, only God knows. I do not believe the *Dutch* intend us
any good by it.

Prop. 9. Problem 6.

How the *Dutch* States may and do underftand Trade better than the Council of State in *England,* or any other.

Subjects, Are the *Dutch* States, and the Council of State
in *England,* or any other.

Queftion. *How the* Dutch *States ?* &c.

Conftruction, By the 11 *Pet.* 2. The *Dutch* States are more
converfant in Trade, and by the 12 *Pet.* 2. The *Dutch* generally breed their Youth of both Sexes more in the Studies
of Geometry, and Numbers efpecially than the *Englifh.* I
fay the *Dutch, ut fupra.*

Ax. 14. For they who are more converfant and better
Educated in any bufinefs may underftand it better than another.

Con-

Construction, But the *Dutch* States are more conversant in Trade than the Council of State in *England* : and the *Dutch* generally breed their Youth of both Sexes better for understanding Trade.

Therefore the *Dutch* States may and do understand Trade better than the Council of State in *England*, or any other.

Apology.

I am so far from intending any diminution by this Proposition to the Regal Authority in this Nation, or any oblique aspersion upon his Majesties Privy Council ; that I do affirm no one thing could conduce more to the grandeur of his Majesty and the publick Interest of the Nation, than to have a constant Council of Trade established by Act of Parliament, which might not only inspect and regulate as well our Native and Forein Trade ; but also be advising and assisting to his Majesty in such Treaties with other Princes and States, wherein Trade is concerned. And how much more this is to be desired, wherein the particular good of every individual person in the Kingdom is concerned, than Corporations, which are advanced to the prejudice of the rest of the Nation, I submit to any indifferent man. And if it be no aspersion upon a Privy Counsellor, who is not a Lawyer, to say in the knowledge of the Laws, the Lawyer may be more understanding ; I do not understand how it can be any to say a Merchant better Educated, and more conversant in Trade, may better understand it, than a Privy Counsellor, who is not so Educated, and less conversant in it.

I say moreover, if all which I have complained of in the former, and this Treatise were regulated, wherein in point of liberty, we were equal with the *Dutch* ; yet if the *Dutch* shall better Govern and Regulate Trade than we, thereby only the *Dutch* may and will drive the Trade of the World exclusive to the *English*.

Prop. 10.

Prop. 10. Theorem 3.

The *Dutch* States govern Trade better than the Council of State in *England,* or any other.

Subjects, Are the *Dutch* States, and the Council of State in *England,* or any other.

Q eſtion, *Whether the* Dutch *States* govern Trade better? I ſay they may.

Ax. 15. For they who may underſtand any buſineſs better than another, may govern it better.

Prop. 7. 2. But the *Dutch* States may underſtand Trade better than the Council of State in *England.*

Therefore the *Dutch* States may and do govern Trade better than the Council of State in *England*, or any other. Which was to be demonſtra ed.

Annotations.

From hence it is that the Trade of *England* is managed confuſedly, diſtractedly, and ſharkingly by the Traders: neither is there any eſtabliſhed Power by which it may be better Regulated: And to this great Wiſdom and underſtanding of the *Dutch* in governing Trade, may be juſtly added ſo great a ſtaidneſs and prudence in all Treaties with Forein Princes and States in reference to Trade, that thereby they have advanced their Trade with all Forein Princes and States: And to this they conjoyn power, by which they, upon all occaſions, improve their Trade above what they had before got by Treaty; which whoſo reads *Leon ab Altzma,* one of their States, may eaſily obſerve.

Prop. 11. Theorem 4.

A Dutch States-man is leſs ſubject to be corrupted to the prejudice of Trade than a Council of States-man in *England.*

Subjects, Are a *Dutch* States-man, and a Counſellor of State in *England.*

Queſtion,

Qeſtion, *Whether the* Dutch *States-man be leſs Subject to be corrupted to the prejudice of Trade?*

I ſay he is.

Ax. 16. For where men are more intereſſed in any Buſineſs, they are leſs Subject to be corrupted to the prejudice of it.

15 *Pet.* 2. But a *Dutch* States-man is more intereſſed in Trade than any *Engliſh* Council of States-man.

Therefore leſs ſubject to be corrupted to the prejudice of Trade. Which was to be demonſtrated.

Annotations.

So as to the great wiſdom and power of the States in governing, is conjoyned Intereſt, whereby their Counſels are eſtabliſhed in greateſt ſecurity, not only ſafe hereby from all poſſible bribery or corruption from any Power from abroad or at home : but this moreover creates a diligence in them all to inſpect the management of all Forein, as well as Domeſtick Trade, whereby as well in the Fiſhing Trade, as in all their Domeſtick Manufactures, their Fiſh and Manufacturos have a reputation incomparably above ours Whilſt our Aulnage, *&c.*

Prop. 12. *Theorem* 5.

Dutch Merchants may and do improve their Trades better than *Engliſh.*

Subjects, Are *Dutch* and *Engliſh* Merchants:

Qeſtion, *Whether the* Dutch *improve their Trades better ?*

I ſay they may.

Ax. 17. For they who have fewer Impediments in any buſineſs, and leſs charge and trouble in it, may improve it better than others, who have more.

Pet. 17. 2. But *Dutch* Merchants have fewer impediments and leſs trouble and charge than *Engliſh* , and have Controverſies in Trade ſooner determined, and with leſs charge.

There-

Therefore with lefs charge *Dutch* Merchants may and do improve their Trade better than *Englifh.* Which was to be !one.

Annotations.

When Controverfies in Trade arife in *England*, it will be firft a very probable queftion, whether the conufance of them belong to the Common Law or Admiralty : Here the Merchant muft wait and intend this bufinefs, whatfoever his concernments are otherways ; if after God knows when the Jurifdiction be determined, then it may be they are removed into the Chancery, where after a tedious delay they may be decreed, and upon a motion, a new Order for re-hearing ; or it may be returned to the Common Law, or perhaps brought into Parliament : and after all this flux and re-flux of vexation and charge to the certain undoing of one or both parties, thefe Controverfies refolve in the determination of men, who it is impoffible, fhould underftand them : for all Judgment is from antecedent Knowledge;and therefore if the nature of Trade,Bills of Exchange, and accounts in Trade, *&c.* and all the particularities which lead to the Controverfies in queftion, be not before underftood, which it is impoffible the Judges in Chancery, Common Law, or Admiralty fhould dó, their Education and Breeding having been otherways, it is impoffible they fhould judge aright.

Propofition 13. *Problem* 7.

How *Dutch* Merchants and their Wives generally underftand Trade better than *Englifh.*

Subjects, Dutch Merchants and their Wives, and *Englifh.*

Queftion, *How* Dutch *Merchants and their Wives generally may underftand Trade better?*

Conftruction. By the 16 *Pct.* 2. *Dutch* Merchants and their Wives are more converfant in Trade, and 12 *Pet.* 2. The *Dutch* generally breed Youth of both Sexes more in the
ftudies

ſtudies of Geometry and Numbers eſpecially. I ſay *Dutch*
Merchants , *&c.* may underſtaod Trade better.

Ax. 14. For they who are better Educated and more
converſant in any buſineſs may underſtand it better.

13 *Pet.* 2. But *Dutch* Merchants and their Wives are generally better educated to underſtand Trade.

16 *Pet:* 2. And are more converſant in Trade.

Therefore *Dutch* Merchants and their Wives generally
may underſtand Trade better than *Engliſh* , which was to
be done.

In all rational deſigns men firſt conſider the end. 2. From
what principles they may attain the end: And thirdly, ſo
to order theſe principles, that the end be attained by feweſt
means aud ſhorteſt ways. The end deſigned by education
of Youth is to live juſtly , to be aſſiſting in Goverment,
and to be helpful to other men. The firſt principle to do
this by education is, that God hath given every Youth underſtanding, as well as ſenſe, to govern all his Actions by
reaſon, not love, hatred, fear, or deſire. 2. That it is in
the power of every learner to do ſomething which is required af him , whereby he may improve his knowledge
by practice. And 3. The means by which Youth is inſtructed is Speech and Method, both which muſt be before underſtood.

To live juſtly is not founded in the principles of Geometry and Numbers; yet this I ſay , that by theſe men are
better enabled to live juſtly than others who are more ignorant in them; for God and Nature hath made all things to
conſiſt in Number and Quantity : that man therefore
who is ignorant herein, though he means juſtly , yet does
not underſtand in his dealings , whether he does juſtly or
not: And in ſo high an eſteem were theſe moſt noble Sciences among the *Grecians* , when Learning flouriſhed ſo
among them that they eſteemed all the world Barbarous
but themſelves , that the greateſt Philoſophers of them,
would

would have all Juſtice and Government to conſiſt in Arithmetical and Geometrical proportion. *Plato* (who would
have all Gods works to be done in Geometrical Proportion, and excluded every one his School who was ignorant
in Geometry *)* though bred in a Democratical State, would
have Juſtice and Government to conſiſt in Geometrical
Proportion. *Xenophon*, though bred in an *Ariſtocratical*,
would have Juſtice to be founded in Arithmetical proportion.

Afterwards *Ariſtotle*, that he might not be leſs a Philo-
ſopher than *Plato*, or *Xenophon* herein, divides Juſtice into Corrective and Diſtributive Juſtice; corrective to be in
Arithmetical Proportion; and Diſtributive in Geometrical:
though for my part I believe he never underſtood one *Prop.*
either in Geometry or Numbers.

1. The ends deſigned by Education in Geometry and
Numbers, are ſuch, that every man by knowledge in them,
is better able to deal in any buſineſs relating to Humane
Converſation, not in Trade only.

The ends of
Education in
Geometry and
Numbers.

2. All fortification is founded in theſe ſtudies, eſpecially
in Geometry : ſo is encamping and approaches, and defen-
ces againſt them. *Archimedes* ſo excelled herein, that when
Marcellus beſieged *Syracuſe*, he alone twice beat back
the *Roman* Army, nor *(*its believed*)* had the *Romans* taken
it, if *Archimedes* had not been ſurprized.

3. Architecture, Surveying, and Meaſuring all Bodies and
Superficies, is wholly founded in them.

4. Aſtronomy is founded in Geometry and Numbers, ſo
is meaſuring the diſtance of places, whereby Navigation is
better to be improved.

5. Hiſtory (which ſo enables the minds of men) is rude
and imperfect without knowledge in theſe Studies, for no
man without underſtanding Numbers can compare *Era's*,
Epocha's, and periods of times, when Actions were done;
nor how they were done in place without Geography, which
is founded in Geometry.

6. Youth by education in theſe Studies, where a method
of Reaſoning is obſerved, does not only acquire by every

Propo-

Proposition a new and certain knowledge, which at some
time or other may be beneficial, but gets a habit of right
reasoning, whereby he is enabled to judg of any Proposition
in any other Science or faculty, and to judge of the reasons
in them.

The Principles   2dly. The Principles of Geometry and Numbers, as of
all Sciences are three, *viz.* Definitions, Petitions, and Axioms, which as I understand, are not rightly underſtood by
Euclid, nor any Commentator upon him: but *Ariſtotle* is ſo
far from understanding the Principles aright, that he does
lib. 1. 10. tit. 3. not underſtand the Number of them: For he ſays *Anal. Poſt.*
& 6. that the Principles of Science are two, Proper, and Com-
lib. 1. c. 3. de mon; Proper, as a Line: Common, as if equals be taken
anima. from equals, what is left will be equal; and the Logick
taught in our Schools eſtabliſhes no Principles at all.

The means.   3dly. The Means by which Youth is inſtructed in Geometry and Numbers, and in all other Learning, is Speech
and Method. Speech is the inſtrument or mean by which
men converſe and inſtruct; our *Engliſh* Tongue therefore
being copious enough to inſtruct Youth in Education, it is
vain and ſuperfluous to do it in any other, where men are
not neceſsitated to ſpeak different Languages: The Greek
and Latin Tongues being the Language of no place, I know
no neceſsity of them, unleſs men deſire to multiply Gods
Curſe in the confuſion of Tongues, by retaining theſe now
there is no neceſsity of them. Yet the better ſort of the
Youth of *England* is condemned to the learning of theſe
tongues, which they at laſt underſtand ſo imperfectly, that
not one of a hundred can ſpeak or know in either ſo well as
his own: and whether this is the neareſt way to Inſtruction,
I leave to any man to judge. The Antient *Egyptians, Syrians,
Caldeani, Grecians,* and *Romans* inſtructed their Youth in their
Mother Tongue, whereby they became ſo eminent in Learning, that this preſent Age enjoyes much benefit from
them.

   The *Affricans* before the Reign of *Manſor* Emperour of
Affrick and all the *Spains*, who reigned, as *Pedro Mexico*
ſays, about the year 1105. were accounted barbarous.
                                                This

This Emperour, being a great lover of Learning , caufed all *Hift. temp.*
Books written in Greek , either concerning Philofophy,
Phyfick, or Hiftory to be tranflated into the *Arabian* Tongue,
and founded many Colledges in the Cities of *Fez, Morocco,*
Affrica, Treviffin, Tunis, Argier, Hippona, &c. and endewed
them with great Revenues for reading thefe Studies in the
Arabian Tongue : whereby not men only, but women fo
profited in Learning, that as *Leo Affricanus* affirms, the women
of *Lybia* in thofe days were very learned, and above all
things elfe, fooner bufied in good Books, than medling with
Cloth and Garments.   And it was in this Emperours Reign,
or foon after, that thofe famous Philofophers, *Averroes, Me-*
fues, Rafis, Rabbi Mofes, and many others flourifhed.   Nor
do I know any reafon, but if Learning were taught Youth in
the *Englifh* Tongue, whereby the *Englifh* might be as learned
as the *Romans,* and *Grecians ,* but the *Englifh* Tongue would
be in as much efteem as the *Greek* and *Latin.*

The Method of Learning in Geometry and Numbers, and
in all other Learning, is by difpofing the knowledge in the
Petitions and *Propofitions* before known; fo the knowledge
what was before underftood to be eternal and neceffary in
the *Axiom,* that the queftion of every *Propofition* not known
before, may neceffarily be known in the conclufion of the
Syllogifm.   But this is impoffible to be done by any Authority of *Ariftotle,* where are no Petitions or mean knowledge
in the Subject ; and thofe Principles which he eftablifhes are
fo confounded, that as he makes a Line to be a Propofition
Principle, fo he makes a man *Anal. Poft.* to be a Univerfal, *lib. 2. c. 19.*
yet a Line is as much a Univerfal as a man :   From whence, as *tit. 7.*
it is impoffible any progref of Learning or Rational Knowledge can follow; fo fuch knowledge as this will. Univer-
fals are every where and cannot be perceived by fenfe, *Ana.*
Poft. l. 1. c. 31. tit. 1.

A Man is a Univerfal.

Therefore a man is every where, and cannot be perceived
by fenfe.

If it be impoffible from Principles thus eftablifhed to learn
or know; then muft it be more impoffible to learn by the
vulgar

vulgar Logick, where are no Principles at all, and all Rules of Learning inverted in the first Definition (as it is called) which sayes Logick proves (not the Consequences but) Principles in its own and other Sciences.

Consequences.

From hence then it is, that in Geometry, is no method observed in Reasoning, whereby the study of it is rendred perplexed and difficult, which is of all others the most natural and easie: The construction of the fourth Proposition, *lib.* 1. is from no antecedent knowledge; and if the negative part of that triangular demonstration be true, which makes two triangle lines to comprehend no space then is all the doctrine of Triangles false; for if a right lined Angle be not space, it is nothing; yet nothing but two right lines comprehend it: And in the vulgar Arithmetick is no reason at all taught; but the learners without understanding any reason are required to divide the Product of the second and third, by the first, and the Quotient will give a fourth proportional number, &c. But how this comes to pass is not understood, whereby learners take no pleasure in learning, and soon forget what was told, without any possible means of improving knowledge in any other Proposition: So as it is from hence that the nobler and better sort of the Youth of *England* being bred up in these vain and fruitless Studies of Grammar, Logick, and Arist. and, being thereby fitted for no Business or Conversations, are disposed to lead idle and debauched lives: and the Female Sex, though it be of mankinde as well as the Male, and endued with a rational soul, and therefore accountable to God and their Superiours for their Actions, are less bred ingenuously in *England*, than in *France, Spain, Italy, Germany*, and the *United Netherlands*, whereby they may be enabled to govern themselves when Virgins and Widows, and to be assisting to their Husbands and Families, when Wives.

I have before often treated by Apology, as well became me, because the King and Laws to which I am Subject were concerned.

cerne'. I need none in what is said upon this Proposition : I have equal right here with any man, and any man with
me. The method prescribed is not four lines , whereby in
Geometry as well as Numbers I will, by Gods leave, from
causes before known , demonstrate the question of every
Proposition not known before: whereas by twenty years
learning of Grammar , Logick , and *Aristotle* this was
never done, nor possible to be done.

Proposition 14. *Theorem* 7.

How *Dutch* Merchants and their Wives generally may govern Trade better than *English* Merchants and their Wives.

Subjects, Dutch *and* English *Merchants and their Wives.*

Question, *Whether the* Dutch *govern Trade better than the*
English ?

I say they may, and do.

Ax. 15. For they who understand any business better may
govern it better.

Prop. 12. 2. But *Dutch* Merchants and their Wives gene-
nerally understand Trade better than the *English.*

Therefore may govern Trade better. Which was to be demonstrated.

Annotations.

From hence it is that *Dutch* Merchants Wives frequently,
when their Husbands are abroad in Trade , or any other business, order and govern their Trades as diligently and dif-
creetly as if they were at home ; which is a very great advantage both to the State and their Husbands , and Families,
and might be of as much, or more to the King and Merchants
here in *England*, if their Wives were so educated , as to be
enabled to do so.

Epilogue.

Epilogue.

SO as Reader thou mayeſt underſtand, and that by demonſtration, in the former Treatiſe from what cauſes, and by what means the *Engliſh* Nation is become ſo degenerate in Strength, Wealth, and Trade. In this thou mayeſt underſtand by what means and degrees the *Dutch* in leſs than 100 years have attained ſuch prodigious Riches and Strength by Trade: we have little left but the *French* and *Canary* Trades (wherein we undo our ſelves) and the Trade of our Manufactures and Plantations. And in theſe two the *Dutch* may out-do the *Engliſh* in Forein Trade, if their charge in acquiring them does not exceed their charge otherways. And herein they may clearly out-do the *Engliſh*, if it be true; which is ſaid, that in them *Engliſh* Factors Trade in their own names, yet upon the account of *Dutch* Merchants; whereby it much more comes to paſs, which Sir *Walter Rawleigh* long ago obſerved, that our Sea and Land Commodities ſerve only to enrich and ſtrengthen other Countries againſt our own.

If we loſe the Trade of *England*, we muſt loſe Navigation; if we loſe Navigation we loſe the Sovereignty of the Seas; if the Sovereignty of the Seas, then read the condition of the Nation in the *Daniſh* Invaſion, and remember it not long ſince. Notwithſtanding the Nation is in this condition, yet are we ſo ingaged in Factions and Diſſentions, that neither the continued ſeries of Gods manifold Judgments theſe many years upon it by Wars Inteſtine and Forein, Plagues, Fires, and Hyrricanoes, nor the growing greatneſs of our Neighbours the *French* and *Dutch*, does any ways alarm or awaken it.

I might

I might here Reader proceed to a third Treatise, by observing the same method, and demonstrate that *England* is capable of greater Wealth, and strength than the *United Netherlands* (or perhaps any Country else) and that, from those natural prerogatives wherewith God hath endued it, the Nation may manage a greater, better, and more valuable Trade upon much less terms than the *Dutch* can a less, worse, and less valuable Trade : But it will be to no purpose to proceed herein, until Trade be relieved, wherein we shewed cause.

The End.